RISE FROM
DARKNESS

RISE FROM DARKNESS

How to Overcome Depression through Cognitive Behavioral Therapy and Positive Psychology

Paths Out of Depression Toward Happiness

Kristian Hall

FAKKEL FORLAG

© Fakkel Forlag AS,
Oslo, Norway
First published in Norway in 2015,
originally titled «Opp fra avgrunnen»

Published in English translation 2016

Translated by: Jonathan Fraenkel-Eidse
Illustrated by: Thomas Nesland Olsen

ISBN: 978-82-999887-3-5

To Dad.
For everything you gave us,
despite your inner darkness.

Contents

God, grant me the serenity to accept the things I cannot change; courage to change the things I can; and the wisdom to know the difference.

– Reinhold Niebuhr

Foreword

My father was an exceptional person. I have never met an adult who was so warm, playful and inventive. It was as though he was taken from a children's tale.

At the same time, he was a person with serious psychological problems which were partly the result of a difficult childhood. He had deep depression and struggled with anxiety. When he was young he self-medicated with alcohol in order to suppress his social anxiety. Eventually this developed into a serious alcohol problem.

He never managed to beat alcoholism, even after he had children. My sister and I grew up in a home where we never knew if Dad was drunk or if he was himself when we came home from school. This resulted in many frightening situations as our mother could not always be there for us.

When I was 14 years old my dad died suddenly. It was a terrible shock for the entire family. Despite his problems, he was a fantastic person who gave me and many others countless warm experiences and memories. I loved him very much, and still do.

My sorrow eventually developed into a deep depression. Full of sorrow and anger, I became a bad person, filled to the brink with negative thoughts and feelings, which in turn made me horrible company for others. One by one I lost most of my friends. They were, quite understandably, not particularly interested in being around me.

I lived in depression for a decade, a depression which continued to grow deeper and which eventually reached a level where my greatest desire was to die. Not a day went by when I did not think of how I would take my life, and when I would do it. The final barrier which kept me from the grave was my love for my mother and sister. When I knew so well what it meant to lose someone in the family, how could I expose them to that again? This became the purpose of my life: to continue to live in order to spare them.

The breaking point for me, the time when the negative thoughts turned, came at the end of my studies when my mother and sister successfully convinced me to seek therapy. They had pestered me about it for years. Eventually I found the courage and sought out the student health service, which quickly set up an appointment with a psychologist.

I was so fortunate to have been assigned an extremely skilled and wise psychologist who, through the use of a combination of psychodynamic and cognitive techniques, guided me through the forest of hurtful memories and negative thoughts and feelings which I had built up over the years. After nearly two years in therapy I had successfully tamed or rid myself of the worst negative thoughts and behavioral patterns, which I had come to think of as my "demons".

Even though therapy was in my case extremely effective and I was free from the desire to die, depression is a stubborn state which can be difficult to overcome entirely. I developed a keen interest in the subject, primarily because I wished to rid myself of my "demons" completely, not just partially. This is why during the past twelve years I have spent much time researching the methods and techniques for taming and curing depression and other psychological illnesses.

The result is that today I am by and large a happy person. I have completely eliminated my depression, *and you can too!* I have a fantastic wife and a sunray of a four-year-old son. My relationships with friends and family can generally be described as close and solid. I have that which I need in terms of material objects, and I live a meaningful life.

My story is by no means unique. Unfortunately, all too many people in the world suffer with depression, anxiety and other psychological illnesses or are generally unhappy. In the USA, 17% of the population suffers from depression during the course of their lives, and it appears as though this may be an increasing problem. In some circles, depression is labeled an epidemic.

At the same time, more and more youths are becoming depressed. Researchers have just begun to uncover what may be the underlying causes of this development. My own theory is that social media such as Facebook makes visible the popular and unpopular to a degree not possible before. It was tough being unpopular when I grew up as well, but it was not nearly so measurable and as public as it is today.

Also, we are being bombarded with images of the beautiful, rich and successful to an extent not seen before. Humans are social beings; we are continually comparing ourselves to those around us. And with social media, there are more of these images to be seen every day, and the images are more polished than ever.

❦

The reason I begin this book with my own story is because it serves as an example, showing that it is completely possible to go from living a "trashed" life to become a functional and happy person. It is possible to rise from the darkness.

One of my goals of this book is for it to communicate hope. Even if you have been stuck with depression for years, it is always possible to improve your life. There are many people before you who have achieved this. How long you have lived with depression or why you are depressed is not so important, as the only thing that counts is how your life can get better. Life is a process; the important thing is which direction you are heading.

My purpose with this book is to give as many people as possible a push on the road to a better life. I believe that this book can be useful to many, as long as they are equipped with a real *desire for change,* meaning that they must be willing to do whatever necessary to feel better. The very first step is to decide to start pulling yourself out of the pit. There is no one else who can do this for you; you must do it yourself.

Imagine the head project leader of NASA, after the American government had decided to send people to the moon. The task must have appeared quite overwhelming, right? The only way to solve such tough assignments is to divide the project into many very small and achievable steps. Afterwards, these steps must be followed, one at a time. The same is true when you wish to overcome depression.

The primary target group for this book is people who struggle with depression, people who are unhappy, and those who care about them. At the same time I believe that this book includes numerous tips that are useful to others, who by and large feel ok and are satisfied with life. Self-improvement is for everyone, not just for those who are down.

Depression is a broad diagnosis which includes thousands of individual conditions. There is no one technique that will help everyone. You must try many things and keep that which works.

It is worth noting here that there is a huge difference between people and their suffering. Some are so depressed that they can barely get out of bed or are even admitted to an institution. Other may be largely satisfied and sometimes happy, but they may feel down now and then. Because situations are so different, not all of the techniques and advice in this book will suit everyone. Keep this in mind while you read. If you feel that something is entirely irrelevant to your situation, skip the chapter and read on.[i]

Some who read this book will be students, others working adults. Many of those who are hit hardest by depression are so sick that they cannot summon the strength to work or go to school or university. It is difficult writing a book to suit all of these different groups, but I have made a whole-hearted effort to do so because I believe that there are numerous important similarities between those who are depressed. I see depression as a staircase: those who are most sick have gone several steps farther down than those who are moderately affected. Yet one can always turn around and begin to climb the steps upward again.

I do not believe that anyone holds the one key to happiness, myself included. But I do believe that humanity holds an enormous collective wisdom. I have attempted to compile some of this wisdom which I have collected from many different sources. You will also find suggestions for further reading at the end of the book.

Regardless of whether you feel ok or utterly horrible right now, I wish you the best of luck in your quest for a better life. I am standing on the sidelines cheering!

Watch your thoughts; they become words.
Watch your words; they become actions.
Watch your actions; they become habits.
Watch your habits; they become your character.
Watch your character; it becomes your destiny.

– (Anonymous)

How to use this book

There are many ways to read a book. Personally, I like to open a new book on page one and plow through it as fast as I can. You can read this book in such a manner, but if you do so, you should read it several times to increase the benefit you receive from it. I have kept the book short. The intention is that you should be able to skim through it in one evening to get an impression of what it's about. You can use a highlighter to quickly go back to those techniques in which you have the most faith.

The core of the book is the techniques. If you want maximum personal change, you need to do the exercises. People learn best by experiencing things directly, not by reading what others have done. Overcoming depression involves teaching oneself to live life in another way, learning how to think differently and to do things which lead to a better balance in one's emotional life.

Whether you read this book quickly or slowly, take the time to try all of the exercises. If a practice does not work for you the first time, try it one more time before moving on. You may find that some of the techniques work perfectly for you, while others do not work at all. Different techniques will work differently from person to person. Use and develop those techniques which are the most effective for you.

Depending on your life situation, some of these techniques may seem pretty tough. I am of the opinion that as a rule it is better to confront our problems, and in doing so to temporarily increase the pain rather than to let the problems continue to produce low-intensity pain over a long period of time. If you are unsure if a technique is right for you, consult with your doctor or therapist.

Another important aspect regarding the exercises is repetition. What you are about to do is to replace old established thought and behavioral patterns with new thoughts and habits which will be more beneficial to you. As with all learning, repetition is the key. You can use electronic tools, such as the app Coach.me (available on iOS and Android platforms, as well as a webpage), to help you to repeat the exercises enough times.

In many of the exercises you will be encouraged to jot down reflections and observations. Therefore, I recommend that you acquire a diary or notebook as soon as possible. Something as simple as this will be one of the most important aids in your battle for a better life.

◊

Coming out of depression can take time. In my case it took more than ten years. It took me so much time because I found that I had to reinvent the wheel; there was no one who gave me a recipe to follow. I hope that you can learn from my experiences, and that you can shorten the time it takes you to get better as much as possible. You can get quite far in a couple of years. How long you need depends on how long you have been depressed and how deep your depression is. Deep and long depressions can lead to changes in your physiology, and it can take some time to reverse it.

This book is built around my own recipe for coming out of depression. The first part, a theory section of sorts, explores how thoughts and feelings are continually affected by mental and emotional filters which, in the case of depressed individuals, make the situations and experiences appear (much) more negative than they actually are. As the main element in my recipe is to eliminate these filters, it is important to understand both what they are and how they work.

If you are really down in the dumps, if every hour is painful, it will be difficult to take serious action and focus on the long haul ahead. What you need in such a case are some simple techniques and activities that can lift your mood[1] a few notches and help your emotional situation just enough that you gain energy to take on the long-term improvement process.

Part 2 of the book is dedicated to this. Here you will find the survival techniques I instinctively used to improve my mood during those years when depression hit me the hardest. In addition, I have found many useful techniques from past decades of psychological research. I find it quite interesting to see that there is a large overlap between "my" techniques and those the professionals describe. Part 2 can be seen as a psychological fire extinguisher – emergency help, here and now.

Part 3 examines those negative conditions which often accompany depression, such as bitterness and anxiety. Sometimes depression is triggered by such states, while other times it is depression which causes them – the classic "chicken and the egg" situation. Whatever the case, it is important to treat them.

When you have gained a little breathing room, prepare to do some heavy lifting, which you will find in part 4. In this phase, which can take several years, you will purposely work with yourself in such a manner that step by step, you become a more harmonious person who lives a better life.

At the end of the book, in part 5, I will describe techniques for meditation and self-hypnosis. These are very penetrating and effective techniques which alone have the potential to make you feel much happier.

&

---

1   The word *mood* is used in this book to refer to the *sum of one's feelings*. To improve one's mood means to gradually introduce more positive feelings: joy, happiness, love and humor. The feelings you must move away from are sadness, melancholy, anger, bitterness and jealousy.

Self-improvement is much easier when you are part of a community. It is useful to have someone to talk with, someone who can understand you and who knows what you are fighting; someone who can motivate you when things are particularly bad. If you do not have friends or family who are capable of or willing to fill this role, you can find forums on the Internet. You can Google "bulletin board depression" to find such forums. There you will find people who know what you are going through.

To those who care about a depressed person

In some cases, it can be quite difficult to be close to somebody who is depressed. It can feel as though you are depressed yourself. Feeling powerless when you see a child, a sibling, a partner, a friend or a parent who is depressed, can be terrible. You only want to help, but often there are few actions that will have a significant effect. It's the depressed person that will need to work themselves out of it. People in the surroundings can support and assist, but not make another person overcome depression.

I believe that one of the most important things that friends and relations can do is to first understand what depression is, and then accept that it is ultimately the person struggling with depression who must decide whether he or she will be become well or not. The most important time in the healing process is when the depressed person actually *decides* to get better. For somebody who is depressed there is often comfort to be found in the depression – they allow themselves to fall back into its familiar embrace. This is one of the reasons depression can last so long.

Nobody, not even parents, can take responsibility for another person's feelings. It can get to the point where the friend or relative must completely resign. If you have tried for years to help without any real effect, then it may be best to take a step back and take a break. By resigning I do not mean that you should give up, but that you can realize that there are limits to how much influence you really can have over another's depression.

On the other hand, what you can continue to do, for as long as necessary, is to encourage a sense of empowerment in the depressed person and to facilitate as many positive experiences as possible; that is to say, everything that can lead to increased production of neurotransmitters which are associated with positive feelings (which we soon will learn more about).

Another thing that will really help is to imagine how the mind of the depressed works; how thought fallacies act. The next part of the book explores this in detail. The depressed will often feel that they are misunderstood, as though nobody understands how they actually feel. It is not surprising that it can be difficult for others to understand, as their thoughts can be completely irrational. Being depressed is a bit like coming from another planet. By understanding false thoughts, you can show that you understand more of the depressed person's world, perhaps making them feel less alone.

Finally, take care of yourself! You cannot help others if you yourself become completely exhausted, anxious or depressed. It is no coincidence that airline flight attendants ask you to first put on your own oxygen mask before you help others.

PART 1
HOW TO BE HAPPY

What is depression?

Many people are depressed without being entirely aware of it. As with most things in life, we are not provided with a manual at birth to tell us what depression is and how to rid ourselves of it.

Depression is not one specific illness; it is an umbrella diagnosis which covers many different situations and conditions. At the core of most depressions lies a persistent sadness, sorrow and melancholy which does not necessarily result from a particular cause or source. Typically, the depressed person will have low energy, require much sleep and may have crying spells and intense psychological pain which may materialize as physical symptoms. Sometimes depression is accompanied by suicidal thoughts. Life can be so painful that one desires to end it.

There are many possible causes for depression. Here are a few of them: traumas from one's childhood or youth, mourning, bullying, low self-esteem, self-criticism and unbalanced chemistry in the body. Some people simply *are* depressed, without a clear explanation as to why.

Many depressed people have a mind full of mechanisms which sustain and amplify the depression. They think negatively about themselves, the world and the future. The key to ridding oneself of depression is to change or eliminate these mechanisms.

A basic principle for me is that being aware of and directing attention to the causes of your depression does not necessarily lead to improvement. Often this may actually exacerbate the problem. People generally do not become happier when thinking of their own pain; quite the opposite, they do so by thinking of those things in life which give them joy and other positive feelings.

What you can change

A person's degree of happiness depends on several factors. Some of them are outside of one's control, such as when a loved one is involved in an accident, or when healthy people suddenly become seriously ill. Accidents can occur randomly and without warning. We cannot choose our parents or which genes we have been given.[ii] Life is in many ways a casino – some win, and some lose.

At the same time, there are people who go through the most horrendous experiences and still manage to maintain a positive mood. Others can fall into darkness from events which to outsiders appear relatively minor.

This book concentrates on those parts of life we have influence over, those which you can change. Improving your life is in many ways about changing your inner life – what you think and feel. Even if it can seem difficult, it is possible to control your thoughts and feelings. These are factors which you do have power over.

The process of going from depression to happiness can be compared to swimming upstream through rapids. The depressed feel as though they are constantly working *against* themselves. But suddenly the current changes direction and they arrive at a situation where they can work *with* themselves. To live in depression is like riding down a self-reinforcing negative spiral. You can turn this spiral around, eventually reaching critical mass, where the self-improvement work almost takes care of itself.

The point at which the spiral turns is what I call the development's "tipping point". Convince yourself that this point exists, and make it your goal to reach it. If you manage this, the rest of the journey is simply taking one step at a time. Remember that the recipe for reaching apparently unreachable goals is to divide them into smaller parts! This is one reason why this book includes so many techniques. Every time you do one of the exercises you will take a step closer to healing. Some of the steps will be sideways, or even backwards, but if you continue to walk, you will ultimately arrive at your destination.

About the brain

Brain activity occurs in two parts: the conscious and subconscious. The conscious is the part of the brain which reads this text and reflects on it. It is the part you use when you decide what you will eat for dinner. This is a simplification, as the subconscious often plays a role in everyday decisions, but this is not important in this context.

The subconscious is the part of the brain that manages automated processes, everything which occurs in the mind and body which we do not have to concentrate on. An experienced driver, for example, does not think through how she[2] will maneuver the car through a corner. This is automatic.

Note that the subconscious used in this context is not the same as that introduced by Freud in his time. Psychology has changed much since Freud's day. The subconscious is nothing more than brain activity you are not aware of.

The brain is made up of roughly 100 billion brain cells.[iii] Each brain cell can on average connect to 7,000 other brain cells, which means that your brain is comprised of several hundred billion so-called synapses, or connections between brain cells.

Whenever you learn something new, these brain cells will come together in synapses and create neural pathways. The

---

2   To simplify the language I alternate between *he* and *she,* instead of writing "he or she." In the same way I often use *work* when I refer to either being a student, studying or going to work. If you do not work, go to school or are not in some form of education, simply replace *work* with whatever you usually do on a day-to-day basis.

more repetitions you do when learning something, the more solid these neural pathways become. All the habits you have acquired exist as neural pathways in your brain. This is also true for bad habits.

Up to 95% of the activity in the brain is comprised of subconscious processes; automated processes which run in the background without requiring one to think about them. Just 5% are conscious thoughts, and this goes a long way to explaining why it can be so difficult to change oneself. As the quote in the introduction suggests, everything begins with a thought, which leads to action, which leads to habits, and habits can in turn dictate much of one's life.

The brain is like a large forest, full of trails. On the trails are wandering many thoughts. Some of the trails are small animal tracks, almost invisible to the untrained eye, while others are almost like highways, full of traffic. In order to change yourself, you must tread new trails and let the forest reclaim those old, well-used roads.

Neural pathways which you do not use disappear. To break bad habits, you must simply do things in a different way.

This is precisely what happens with neural pathways which are not used – they will gradually dissolve. Once upon a time I was relatively good at advanced calculus. Today I can hardly remember any of it. I have never had use for that knowledge and therefore have not used those neural pathways. In the same way I have completely rid myself of the internal criticism which had plagued me earlier, by toning down the criticism and eventually eliminating it completely.

To get rid of unfavorable thought and behavioral patterns which physiologically exist as neural pathways you wish to dissolve, you must stop using these neural pathways. *You must unlearn what you have learned.* Then they will gradually disappear on their own.

The best and fastest means to achieve this is by learning how to think, feel and act in new ways. There are many roads to Rome, mentally and emotionally. The work begins by identifying the thought and behavioral patterns you need to get rid of, which we will examine more closely later in the book.

What are feelings?

Have you ever thought about what feelings are, and how they occur? This will be important knowledge for you in the days to come as you learn to increase your control over them. Biologically speaking, feelings are an important part of the body's information system.

The brain can send signals to the body's cells via two systems: the nervous system and the so-called endocrine system. You are certainly familiar with the nervous system; it is what makes you feel pain when you hurt yourself. The endocrine system produces and manages the body's hormones.

The nervous system is in charge of all fast communication in the body, a typical response takes just nanoseconds, while endocrine responses can last between a few hours and several weeks. The endocrine system is involved in many important processes in the body such as the immune, reproductive and digestive systems.

Both the nervous and the endocrine system are based on chemistry. The nervous system is based on electrochemistry; information is sent as an electric signal, which is transmitted between nerve cells via molecules called neurotransmitters. The endocrine system is exclusively based on chemistry. Hormones are relatively large molecules, produced by different glands in the body and the brain, and which are transported via the body's various fluids (such as blood and lymph fluid) to the body's cells. In addition to hormones, neurotransmitters are important to the body's signal systems. We can call hormones and neurotransmitters signal substances as they function as the body's messengers, sending messages from one part of the body to another.

You may have heard of neurotransmitters like serotonin and dopamine, as well as hormones like endorphins and adrenaline. These are just some of the substances which the brain produces in order to communicate with the rest of the body. The primary function of these substances is to tell the cells what they should do. Author Joe Dispenza observes that *thoughts are the brain's language, and feelings are the body's language.*

In addition to signal substances functioning as the brain's messenger to the rest of the body, your conscious and subconscious self will have a concrete experience of these substances. If your body is full of endorphins, you will feel positive, energetic and happy. If you have too little serotonin and dopamine in your system, you may feel depressed.

To improve your mood, you must change the chemical balance in your body. This is done by making the brain and other glands (such as the adrenal, thyroid and pancreas) produce another mix of signal substances: less of those signal substances associated with negative feelings, and more of those that make you happier. In practice this means that, among other things, you must increase the production of serotonin, endorphins and oxytocin. Research shows us which activities lead to the increased production of these substances. This is why later in the book I encourage you to dance, sing, exercise, be in nature, meditate and smile. All of these activities lead to mood improvement by changing the production of the body's signal substances.

Because the signal substances are chemistry and the constituents of these substances come from that which we drink and eat, it is important to be aware of our diet. Unbalanced diets can lead to an imbalance in the body's chemistry, which can then lead to imbalance in the production of signal substances, which in turn can lead to negative emotions.

You can be happy and at the same time have the worst diet in the world, as diet is simply one factor among those which can affect emotions. But if you are suffering from depression or other types of unbalanced emotions, it is a good idea to cross off 'bad diet' as a potential contributing factor.

Reality filters

Thoughts and feelings are interrelated, as with the "chicken or the egg" metaphor. If you are depressed, it can be difficult to think positive thoughts; the negative feelings pull the mental processes down into darkness. At the same time, negative thoughts cause the body to produce signal substances which lead to negative feelings.

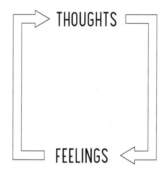

Both thoughts and feelings are affected by numerous layers of mental filters before they end up creating a concrete experience in the mind. That which we experience subjectively is a result of an interpretation process in the brain. When we look at something, the lenses in our eyes invert the image such that it is projected upside-down at the backs of our eyeballs. The signals are then sent to the brain via optical nerves and the brain's thalamus, to be interpreted by the vision center in the brain. In the end we experience the situation "right-side-up".

This is how it is with all sensory impulses we receive. Everything is taken in by the brain and interpreted before we experience the impulse. Because different people have different mental filters, one situation will never be experienced in the same way by different people. Take arachnophobia for example. If two people see a large spider and only one of them has arachnophobia, the experiences of each person will be entirely different. In this example, the phobia is the filter.

Here is another example: Imagine two people, Jon and Sue, who meet a third person, Joanna. If Jon believes that all people are wicked and Sue believes all are good, they will interpret what Joanna says in very different ways. They will see and experience Joanna completely differently.

We have such filters for most things in life. They are an important reason why people quarrel so much. We continually fall into the trap of believing that others see the world in the same way as we do. This is rarely the case – just think of how differently the world must be experienced by a blind person, a deaf person, and a person who has both their sight and hearing intact. Think about how differently men and women can see the world, or children and adults – or how differently a communist and a CEO see things. Reality is subjective.

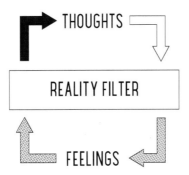

I call these mental and emotional filters "reality filters," a concept which comes from the psychologist Timothy Leary and was later further developed by the philosopher and author Robert Anton Wilson. They called the phenomenon *reality tunnel*; I prefer "reality filters."

The American psychologists Karen Reivich and Andrew Shatté refer to this as *iceberg beliefs* and write about it in the excellent book *The Resilience Factor*. They use the iceberg metaphor because these beliefs lie under the surface and often are much more extensive and influential than they appear at first sight.

◊

We all live with one or more reality filters. We need them in order to relate to a chaotic and complicated world. Reality filters allow us to simplify things, to sort impulses and impressions into known patterns. The problem arises when the reality filters warp reality in a negative direction.

A neo-Nazi can believe that black people are of less worth than white people, or that Jews are responsible for an international conspiracy. A radical communist can believe that all capitalists are evil.

What do you believe? Maybe you believe that everything that happens to you happens because you are especially unlucky, or that it is impossible that anyone could love you. If this is the case, imagine how much better your life could be if you could exchange that perspective.

What we believe often comes true. Robert Anton Wilson summarized it like this: "What the Thinker thinks, the Prover proves." He is referring to our tendency to search for and find proof for that which we believe in, no matter what it may be. For example, it is not difficult for a climate skeptic to find "proof" that climate change is not caused by humans. Neither is it difficult for apocalyptic cultists to find proof that the end is near. If you believe that people cannot be trusted, you will note everything that supports this belief while ignoring all indications that the opposite is true.

Reivich and Shatté refer to this phenomenon as the Velcro/ Teflon effect. That which supports our convictions fastens like

Velcro, while that which contradicts them slides off as if coated in Teflon.

Reality filters are created during our childhood and are developed by the things we learn from the people around us: relatives, daycare staff, teachers and so on. If we grow up in an environment where gay people are seen as less valued than others, the chances are that we will end up with the same opinion ourselves.

These filters are made up of, among other things, your political and religious views and your general view of humanity. They are also made up of your values and principles. Furthermore, they are made of your self-image and self-confidence.

As we have seen, reality filters are in principle a neutral phenomenon, one which can have favorable, neutral or unfavorable effects on your emotions. For depressed people, unfavorable reality filters are an important part of the illness. A depressed person, for example, will often misinterpret communication from others, often in a negative sense.

By having a good understanding of your own reality filters makes life much simpler. It makes it much easier to understand why you react the way you do to the things that happen to you. It is tiresome to constantly try to keep up with yourself, and to deal with reactions that appear illogical, even to you.

Through awareness, you will be able to identify which reality filters make you feel unwell and ensure you continue to be depressed. When you have identified these, you can begin working on changing or eliminating them. If you can manage to do this, you have come a long way out of depression.

Reality filters which distort impulses and thoughts, and which create painful emotions, can be seen as mental "demons." We will take a closer look at these in the next chapter.

Demons and thought fallacies

Thoughts and feelings can end up in locked patterns and habits. The reason for this is that thoughts run along the neurons which are made in the brain. They take the path of least resistance, preferring to follow the brain's highways. In doing so, they make the roads they travel wider. They are self-reinforcing by nature. The illustrator of this book, who is also a friend of mine, refers to this as a bicycle track. Imagine a cyclist who is biking in a circle over and over again. In time, a deep track is created which the

> I define demons as thought patterns or habits which lead to behavior that does not benefit you, or to negative emotions. A demon is a rotten reality filter.

bicycle will follow. The longer the time, the harder it is to steer in another direction.

Some of these patterns are beneficial, such as when we brush our teeth before going to bed. Other patterns and habits can be extremely disadvantageous. It does not harm anybody if you prefer to eat breakfast before you shower (or vice versa). Yet the thought patterns of depressed people directly or indirectly lead to depression, sadness and a poor ability to function in society. I refer to these thoughts and behavior patterns as demons.

Demons can manifest themselves in several ways, both conscious and subconscious, such as when you get an urge to revel in unhealthy food when you get upset, or when you believe that nobody could love you because you have been rejected by somebody of the opposite sex. Other demons function as a voice of inner criticism inside the mind.[iv]

Note that this is a metaphor. I am not writing about demons such as those found in films like *The Exorcist*. I am referring to parts of *your own psyche* which do not benefit you, not a creature which comes from the outside and takes control. You can see these demons as the small red devils in cartoons, which sit on the shoulder and whisper bad advice. I am not referring to biblical demons, but to purely psychological ones.

This is a relatively complex concept, which is best explained through examples. The following is an everyday example, followed by a more serious situation.

One day you are called in by your boss for a meeting. The boss is satisfied and commends you for the work you have done recently. By and large, he has only positive things to say. Nevertheless, at the end of the conversation he mentions one area that requires improvement. He thinks that you could be better at giving constructive feedback to your colleagues, as you can be a little negative in the department meetings.

You leave the meeting with a bad feeling. You do not consider for a second all of the commendations you have just received, but think only of the last comment; that you are negative with your colleagues. *There goes that promotion,* you think. *The boss sees me as a negative element at the office.* The rest of the day you are in a bad mood, and you are miserable when you get home from work. You end up in a fight with your spouse, and you snap at your children because they have not done their homework.

This is an example of a relatively mild demon: focusing on the negative in a situation and ignoring the positive. Now for the other example:

Imagine that you are on your way to a party where there are many people you do not know. You enter the party venue and immediately get a bad feeling. You feel that people are looking at you with skepticism, or almost hostility. You sense a lump in your stomach, a well-known fear which increases with every passing minute. The fear gives way to panic and you look frantically around for somebody you know, yet no one can be found. They probably have not yet arrived.

Now, luckily you spot an old acquaintance, Robert. You go over to him. He is standing in a circle of people you have never seen before, and they look at you with irritation as you interrupt their conversation. Robert greets you, but is clearly irritated also. This is the last straw, so you excuse yourself and quickly leave the apartment and the party.

On the way home you flay yourself for having ruined yet another party, for again having failed to deal with a social event. You are totally incapable, you say to yourself, you should simply go and hang yourself. You are worthless! You go home and lie down in bed, taking with you a deep depression which remains throughout the long, dark night.

The above example is written from the 'protagonist's' perspective. Yet had Robert been asked about the incident the following day, he would have said he was glad to see the protagonist, and that it was unfortunate that he had left so soon. Robert was not irritated in the slightest; he was simply in the middle of a story when the protagonist showed up. In the protagonist's perspective, this was interpreted as irritation and rejection.

I believe that this is a relatively typical example of how social anxiety and depression can occur. The above example shows how demons can change everything you experience, color everything in dark hues and transform all things positive to negative. It also shows how dangerous demons can be, how they can utterly destroy lives. A lot of people go through such experiences many times each and every day.

Demons are found in the subconscious and are formed in the aftermath of one or more past experiences. They can, for example, come from an assault or other traumatic childhood experience. Some demons originally begin as beneficial thought patterns which later spin out of control. A good example of this is worries. If you never worry, the chances of being injured in an accident increase. In this way, worries are good. But if you spend several hours every day worrying about everything that can theoretically occur (and which almost never occurs), these worries have become a demon. It was made to help, to support or to defend you, but then it became twisted and mutated over time – and suddenly it was no longer a helper, but a torturer.

Another way of seeing this phenomenon is to view it as a "machine in the brain". We all have 'machines' in the brain, which produce different things. For example, we have a calculating machine, which produces more or less accurate answers to mathematical problems. We have communication machines which produce more or less effective communication in verbal or written form. Clearly this is also a metaphor – there are no gears in the brain, but there are specialized neural pathways which have particular purposes, which remember things, control the body, reason and so on.

In the depressed, however, one may find machines which are effective producers of things like sadness, despair, bitterness, jealousy and low self-image. These machines function perfectly in principle – they can produce enormous amounts of the products they are configured to produce. The problem is that the products are wrong. But we can reconfigure the machine so that it produces another product. Or we can turn it off.

We can defeat demons and become stronger and wiser in the process. The first thing you must do is to be aware of the demons – get to know them. Afterwards you must accept their existence in order to create a strategy to defeat them. In the end a plan is implemented, resulting in a situation where the demon no longer holds the same degree of power, or where it is gone forever. This provides a feeling of mastery, which in turn gives courage and energy to push on with the work.

Mastery, willpower and self-confidence are central concepts when hunting demons. This process will certainly include some defeats and disappointments along the way. You do not win every battle you engage in. To build a better version of yourself is a little like playing *Snakes and Ladders:* you fall down a level or two every so often, but also find ladders which provide a substantial jump upward.

Perseverance and decisiveness will be important personality traits in this process. Do not lose heart if these are currently not your strongest traits, because this book includes techniques to strengthen them. The trick is to build up self-confidence and willpower slowly but surely through the mastery of those challenges you currently have the ability in which to succeed. It is a little like high-diving – a novice does not begin on the highest diving board. In the same way, try to not take on too much in the beginning, but instead start slowly and equip yourself with time and patience. A good strategy is to endeavor to win many small victories over time, while not allowing the small defeats to knock you out of the battle. If you have a head full of demons, you probably have had them for some time. You will manage holding out for a few years, as long as you know that you are moving in the right direction.

If you visit a professional therapist, it is quite unlikely that they will use the term *demon,* even if they understand what the patient is talking about. Cognitive psychologists will rather speak of flawed ways of thinking, which I refer to as thought fallacies. I see thought fallacies as that which the demon is built of.

The reason I insist on using the word *demon* is that in many cases the phenomenon can have an enormous impact on one's life. This is not simply a little annoying tendency to have negative thoughts, but instead refers to inner problems which can completely paralyze and destroy a life.

In the 60s and 70s the American psychologists Aaron Beck and Albert Ellis developed what we today know as cognitive behavioral therapy (CBT). The core of CBT is to understand how you think, and how you can change this way of thinking over time so that you get to experience an improved quality of life. One searches specifically for disadvantageous thought patterns, which can be called thought fallacies. There are many good books on CBT, and I especially recommend *Change Your Thinking with CBT* by Sarah Edelman. It is full of examples of different thought fallacies, making it easier to understand which thought fallacies you have. Here is an overview of the most important types:

Generalizing

We generalize all the time. In many cases this is fine. Saying that 'all cats are sweet' is quite harmless, even if this is obviously not always the case. But thoughts like 'I never succeed at anything' or 'everyone I know is an idiot' represent damaging generalizations.

"Should-ing"

In my world the word *should* is one with little usefulness. It is a judging word which says that there is something you should have done but did not, or vice versa. It is a word which inevitably carries with it a bad conscience. *I should exercise, I should eat less candy, I should visit my mother more often.* In this book you will not find the word *should* often. It is fine being aware of what actions are appropriate, but constantly going around with a bad conscience is of little use. "Should-ing" is fortunately relatively easy to eliminate. Simply exchange the word *should* with *can* in all situations. *Can* is a word which opens up possibilities and holds no form of judgment, such as that found in *should*.

Over-dramatizing

It is normal for people to over-dramatize the negative things they experience such as receiving a parking ticket. It is irritating to get parking tickets, and sometimes people do not have the money to pay the fine, but they do not represent the end of the world. Over-dramatizing is what you do when you take a negative incident and inflate its significance.

Polarizing

The world is not divided into black and white; rather, different phenomena and events occur along a gray scale. Just the same, many of us insist on sorting things into just two categories, that is to say polarizing, for example, by dividing people into either *good* or *bad* categories. This is a gross oversimplification. All attributes are distributed along scales – it is not as though a person is either funny or completely devoid of humor. Nor is someone either completely evil or totally good.

Personalizing

This thought error refers to taking responsibility for something that occurs, even though it is not your responsibility. Personalizing is not recognizing the wise words of Reinhold Niebuhr at the beginning of this book (read them again). There are many things that happen, both good and bad, which are completely or partially out of our control. Life can get quite heavy if you go around taking responsibility for everything that happens. One example of this thought fallacy is when a friend is in a bad mood, and you believe that it is your fault. We cannot take responsibility for others' feelings.

Blaming

Blaming is the opposite of personalizing. This is what we do when we blame external forces or people for something, when we hold partial responsibility for that which has happened. The truth usually lies somewhere in between these two extremes. Always blaming others makes you blind to the fact that the real problem sometimes lies with you. An example is a worker who arrives late every day at the office, and then blames the boss when they get fired for it. Another is when a partner leaves due to the other's infidelity, and the unfaithful partner insists that it was the other which drove them to it.

Mind reading

We often go around believing that such-and-such a person thinks such-and-such about us, and more often than not it is something negative. *She doesn't like me,* one can think. We often make such conclusions based on misinterpretations of expressions or body language. Maybe the person in this example had a bad day the last time they met, and for this reason was not especially friendly. To conclude that *she does not like me* because of this is mind reading, and it is a useless way of thinking.

Filtering

People with depression have a tendency to latch on to the negative in a situation. They filter information, straining out the positive and ending up with a soup of negativity – like a teenager with nearly straight A's on his report card getting hung up on the one C, or the hostess who believes the whole dinner is ruined because she burned the cake. Unfortunately, they will then make the situation much worse by throwing over-dramatizing into the mix. Not only was the dinner ruined, but her husband will hate her for it and leave her.

Put aside the book for a moment, and think about some incidents you have experienced lately. Can you recognize some thought fallacies you have made? If the answer is yes, jot them down in a notebook or journal. To eliminate the thought fallacies you make, you must first know what they are.

PART 2
GET BETTER RIGHT NOW

A toolbox for
a better life

With the help of personal experience and by reading many books, I have built up a library of techniques and methods which can help ease the pain.

We are all different, and it is not a given that what works for me will work for you. At the same time, I am convinced that you will find techniques which can be useful – as long as you do them with gusto! Try out as many techniques as possible; keep and develop those which give you something. Build your own toolkit.

Depression rarely moves in straight lines. It goes up and down, and back and forth. You can have good days and especially bad days. You can have a long period where things go quite well, before again falling into a black hole which can last for months. Some techniques are better suited to a particular phase; there are techniques for relatively good days and others for the worst of days. The only way to find out how they work for you is by trial and error.

I find comfort in knowing that most everyone goes through tough periods during the course of their lives. This is not because I wish the people around me ill, but because *everybody hurts* – because having it rough is a part of being human. You are never alone. There are no situations that at least one other person has not experienced and emerged from in some manner.

Ask yourself the question: *Is there anybody out there who has had my condition or illness, but who has rid themselves of it and today lives a happy life?* I know of many people who have had a miserable life, but who have then emerged out of the tough times. I am one of them.

Not only is it normal to suffer; it is necessary in order to experience the good in life. As a rule, things are defined by their opposites, like yin and yang. It is difficult to value happiness and prosperity without first knowing what it is like to suffer or to be impoverished.

There will likely be several people in your circle who, either in part or in full, understand what you are going through. Try to find them, dare to talk to them about it. If there are no such people around you, or if you do not have deep enough relationships where it is natural to speak of such problems, find an online community.

Another source for meaningful community is open groups organized either by the public sector or private initiatives. Alcoholics Anonymous, for example, has decades of experience helping people rid themselves of alcoholism. There are similar groups for people with anxiety, depression and other types of addictions and so-called co-addiction, a state one can end up in when living with a person with addictions. There are also grief support groups, where you can meet others who have experienced loss.

Imagine the thousands of people who have gone through what you are experiencing, standing at the finish line of a marathon cheering, and where you are the one running. They are the living proof that intense physical or mental pain need not last forever. It is hard to run and maybe there is still some distance to go, but there is an end to the pain, and that is where you are heading.

A crash plan

What follows is a plan for getting through the worst days or weeks. It is based on a situation where you feel so bad that you cannot summon the strength to go to work.

If you are able to work (or go to school/university), doing so is a big advantage as it will help to reduce the focus on the pain. You meet colleagues and maybe friends at work, and having company around often eases the suffering when you are in pain. Even a few hours are better than staying at home the entire day. If you do not have a job, you can replace work by meeting a friend or with activities.

Time is working for you. Divide the day into smaller parts, and get through each of them. Get through the day, the week and eventually the months. Things will get better.

- *Get up when you awaken.*
  If you have a tendency to sleep in (depressed people have a greater need for sleep than others), set the alarm clock and get up at around 10 o'clock, for example. Get as many hours awake as possible during daylight. It is probably better for you to get up even if your body and mind are screaming for you to remain in bed. If you stay in bed all day it will be difficult to sleep in the evening, and at night the pain will be more intense. You probably will not be able to sleep more than 12 hours per day, and it is much better to be awake during daylight than during the night. It will also help to be together with other people, something which is more difficult to do in the middle of the night.

- *Tidy up your accommodations, and give them a good scrub if necessary.*
  Mental hygiene begins with clean surroundings.

- *Take a shower.*
  You will feel refreshed and have more energy for the other points in the plan. A shower or bath feels cleansing. Put on clean clothes that you associate with good memories – do not go around in pajamas or sweats.

- *Eat breakfast, and eat as healthy food as possible.*
  Try to eat regularly and as healthily as possible, even if your appetite is non-existent. Blood sugar levels affect mood, and this is one of the factors you can control. If you absolutely cannot manage to eat a meal, force down a handful of nuts. Nuts are an energy-rich food, bursting with nutrients.

- *Go for a long walk, preferably somewhere in nature.*
  Listen to uplifting music that you know improves your mood. Get outdoors often. Go on walks. This will expose you to daylight, and you will get exercise, and both will improve your mood. You are in motion, something which may help change the way you think.

- *Eat lunch (healthy food).*

- *Do something distracting.*
  If you are able to and have the desire, meet up with friends, family or acquaintances. Being together with others will make it easier to think about things other than your own pain. Meeting at others' homes can also help as a change in your surroundings also makes it easier to think about something else. Alternatively, you can watch a funny, exciting or uplifting movie or play videogames.

During the worst phase, it's about passing time because time equates to pain. Find out what is most distracting, and spend a lot of time on this.

If your problem is anxiety or the like, you must think a little differently. If you have frayed nerves, videogames, exciting books and movies may increase the anxiety level when what you need is peace. Instead, seek out nature or people that have a calming effect on you.

- *Eat dinner (healthy food).*

- *Make a new attempt at doing something distracting.*
  In the final hours before you go to bed, try to avoid activities that make it more difficult to sleep, such as exciting books/movies or videogames.

- *Go to bed when you are tired.*
  If you cannot sleep, get up and try again later when you are feeling more tired.

Therapy

If you are suffering from deep depression, you may well need professional help. There are many skilled therapists out there whose job it is to help you.

Unfortunately, there are many people who could lead a better life with the help of therapy, but who do not seek it out. Typical excuses are: *Therapy is good for some, but I do not need it.* Or: *One day I will begin therapy, but not now.* Others have economic arguments against therapy. While therapy is relatively expensive, look at it in the bigger context: How much is it worth to be rid of or to reduce your mental suffering?

In my case, my sister and mother pestered me for years before I took this step. Finally finding the courage to seek help was one of the most important elements in my own healing. If I had sought out therapy earlier, I could have saved myself several years of suffering.

If this applies to you (be honest now), think about it: What do you have to lose aside from the money? You can try and see if it works. No matter what happens, it will be an interesting experience.

I am not an expert in clinical psychology, but allow me to give you some advice based on my own experiences:

Tell people around you that you are ill. The period ahead of you can be the toughest in your life, and you will need all the support and encouragement you can get. You need not be afraid of using your network for this; the people around you will generally be happy to be able to help. If you do not have relationships which lend themselves to this, seek out a public discussion group.

Be patient. The results will not likely be evident during the course of the first few consultations. You are fighting against mental demons which have spent years establishing themselves. You may need several years to remove them. But you will succeed!

Do not bite off too much at a time, especially if you have had a traumatic childhood or suffered from a bad event in the past, such as abuse or violence. Take one thing at a time; open the lid just enough so that you can move on without being completely knocked down by what lies beneath the lid.

Contribute to the therapy. Effective therapy is entirely dependent upon the clients sharing themselves willingly and openly. It is you who must do the work; the therapy simply shows the way. *Let go* when you are sitting on the chair or lying on the couch. Let your mouth talk without trying to control what it says.

If you do not find the right chemistry with your therapist, try to find another. Therapists are also people, and we do not always get along with everyone we meet. Personally, I had a very good experience with my first therapist, but when I met a second therapist years later, I ended up cancelling the therapy after two sessions due to bad personal chemistry.

There are several different approaches within psychotherapy. I recommend finding a therapist who is skilled in both cognitive and positive psychology (ask how the therapist works). Cognitive therapy is concerned with eliminating thought fallacies. Positive psychology aims to improve the mood with the help of techniques which produce positive feelings. The techniques in this book borrow from both of these approaches.

A final note: Defeat the shame! There is no shame; there are many who are experiencing this, just like you.

Chimney sweeping

Chimney sweeping (catharsis) is emptying oneself of negative thoughts and feelings, and loosening emotional knots. When getting to know yourself better, it can be useful to first empty yourself entirely – to push reset. Chimney sweeping is a sort of ritual cleansing, where you get ready for the healing phases which will follow.

This step is not necessary for everybody. If you spend hours of your day thinking about how bad you feel, skip this chapter, as you do not need further exposure to the pain. Chimney sweeping is most important for those who are down or depressed without really knowing why, and for those with a history of trauma and intense negative experiences that they are struggling to unlock. If your feelings are unclear or are blended together in a complicated soup, this can work for you. Chimney sweeping can also be useful in processing grief.

There are several methods of chimney sweeping. The most common method is to talk oneself dry. Many do this instinctively. When life is tough, they will call their best friend or a close family member and talk out all of the pain.

The disadvantage with this variant is that those confided in are generally somebody you know which means that you may hold back, or alternatively speak too freely about conflict-causing themes, which can end up creating relationship issues. This problem can be solved by paying someone to listen, someone you do not know such as a psychologist, a coach or a religious leader (the latter will often do this for free).[3] This is one of therapy's most important functions – we all need to empty ourselves from time to time.

Crying is another alternative. If you cannot cry on your own, try the following method: make sure that you are completely alone. Put on sad music. Turn off the lights and light a few candles. If you have lost somebody, place a few pictures of that person on the table. If not, think of something that makes you really sad, or put on a tragic film. Engulf yourself in sorrow. Do not fight the tears if they come; let them run freely. With a little training you will be able to cry at will. Afterwards, you will feel relaxed and empty. It is a strange and rather comforting feeling.

As an alternative, one can also use anger. But this should be pursued with a degree of caution. Some people have so much pent-up aggression that they can lose control when it is first let loose. I will therefore not recommend this method if you are not relatively familiar with how you react to your fury. And I will definitely advise against this method if you have a history of acting violently toward others. This alternative is best if you feel that you are stuck with your own feelings, and when your situation is characterized by passivity.

If you have never tried this before, do it alone. Take a walk in the forest alone, for example. When you have arrived at a suitable place, find a big stick. Then begin to growl, low at first, then increasingly louder. Imagine everything you are angry at in the world – all the people you are angry with and all the situations which have made you feel humiliated and trampled on. Then let loose. Scream and yell until you lose your voice. Hit your stick around you and imagine you are crushing all obstacles. When your anger gradually dissipates, you will feel a similar feeling to that felt after crying, an exhaustion which feels good.

---

3   I admire Catholicism's opportunity to confess. They really understand the chimney sweeping concept. We all need this.

Hard training which leads to physical exhaustion can also be used as a form of chimney sweeping. Or you can use creative expression: Take a blank piece of paper and draw how you feel.

Choose the alternative which works best for you, and continue chimney sweeping until you feel completely empty. You can do one session a day, or maybe just every weekend. Depending on where you stand today, it can take anywhere between a few days and a few months before you reach a state of complete emptiness – where you have really blown out all of the old crap. Then you are ready to move on.

The Diary

A diary is an excellent aid to chimney sweeping. It is always available, and it is private. In other words, you can write things in the diary which might otherwise be embarrassing to tell to your closest friend or therapist.

Make a habit of writing in your diary when you are in pain, but also write on good days. Writing thoughts and feelings will ease the pain. It can have the same effect as talking with someone about the problem; it empties you of dammed-up pain and frustration. The difference is, as mentioned above, you avoid censoring yourself; you can write whatever you want. In addition, the diary is always available, which is not always the case with people.

Diaries are an invaluable tool for mapping the illness as well as logging the process of getting better. You can begin right now. Put down this book and find something you can write on and with. Start on the first page and simply write. Do not think about what you are writing; simply "let the words flow." You can, for example, begin to write what you feel right now, and why you think you feel that way. You can write a little about what you desire in life. Write yourself dry. Observe how you feel afterwards compared to before you began to write.

Live here and now

"Live here and now" is a cliché, you might say. I am not afraid of using clichés. Clichés are life wisdom that has been passed down through the generations, mantras that are repeated so often that sometimes they lose their power. We often take clichés for granted and do not always reflect on their meaning.

"Live here and now" is maybe the most valuable cliché of all. But this can be difficult for many of us to do in practice. We are so used to rolling along the highway of life that we rarely really live in the now.

Put down this book and lean back. Listen to the sounds around you. Try to feel how your body *actually* feels. Feel where in your body you have tension, and which parts of the body are relaxed. Notice your breathing, how quickly you breathe, how evenly you can breathe in and out. Breathe slowly and deeply. Look at the space around you; notice the color nuances and textures on the walls, the details in all the objects present. Are there people around you? Observe them without doing anything yourself. Are there smells in the room? Try to describe them. Take a few minutes using all of your senses to register the details of your surroundings and inside you.

Did you notice that plaguing thoughts, plans and worries disappeared for a moment? That for a moment they ceased to exist? That was quite pleasant, was it not?

The most important signal that you are actually present in the here and now is that you stop thinking. This is not always easy to accomplish. Many experience thoughts as their own perpetual motion machines, like water mills of ideas, problems, worries and plans.

> Mental pain is often connected to either the past or the future: traumas and grief of the past, and worries to the future.

What is needed is practice. Everything begins with deciding to live in the now, and trying a few times each day to slow down the tempo a little bit more each time. With training you can eventually achieve a state where time is irrelevant, where it actually ceases to exist. At this point you are really present, living in the here and now.

One of the reasons that I write about this is that living in the here and now reduces the pain one feels when one is living with depression, anxiety, grief or other emotionally difficult life situations. With enough training you can eliminate the pain entirely. When you are 100 percent present in the moment, when time disappears, when there is no longer a past or a future, it is virtually impossible for the mental pain to exist.

The art of living in the here and now is really a meditation technique. The simplest way for a beginner to reach this presence in the now is to bring it about through meditation. In the final part of this book you will find a meditation technique which can be used for this purpose.

As John Lennon so wisely put it, "Life is what happens while you are busy making other plans." Life is nothing more than a *series of moments*, affected by the past and with dreams and plans for the future. It can be advantageous to tone down the past and the future, and to concentrate on the moment.

One branch of philosophy which I highly regard is an offshoot of Buddhism called Zen. Zen Buddhism is, to me, more of a lifestyle than a religion. Modern ideas like mindfulness have borrowed much from Zen Buddhism. Through meditation and concentration, one seeks to experience the moment without interference from the past and the future. There are no good or bad moments in Zen, just moments, and you can seek oneness with the moment, no matter what it may be.

If you live according to Zen's principles, you will try to enjoy boring situations as much as you enjoy watching a good movie or another experience. This can be worth considering the next time you do the laundry or mow the lawn. Try to listen intensely to the sounds around you, see the variations in the light in your surroundings, take in the smells, and notice what you taste.

One concrete technique for practicing this ability is to try to discover new details in your immediate surroundings. Next time you take a walk around the neighborhood, try to find at least five details you have not noticed before. This may be a beautiful tree in the neighbor's yard, a special window on the top floor in a block, an advertisement with a funny pitch or an unusual color combination in the clothes of a person passing by. If you find it difficult finding new details, lift your sights – above there are many things you have not seen before.

Bring on the good feelings

If what you are feeling right now is frustration, grief, depression or anger, it can be difficult to imagine basking in good feelings. But it is possible for everyone, even for the unhappiest among us, to change feelings in a positive direction.

We humans have different triggers for positive and negative emotions. It is important to identify these triggers, so that you can search for the positive and avoid the

Find out what makes you happy and spend as much time on it as possible. At the same time, avoid negative triggers.

negative. The recipe for this is actually quite simple: it's about trying lots of different things and keeping whatever works. It can also be a good idea to note how you react to different activities and then it will be easier to discover the patterns.

The techniques in this chapter result in the increased production of signal substances associated with better moods. At the same time, you will become aware of your own triggers. With better awareness, you can gradually change your habits and do more of that which makes you happy and less of that which makes you depressed.

Laugh

Look at your life situation as a gigantic joke. Laugh at it. If things are falling apart, look at yourself from the outside and laugh out loud. Look at your situation from a cosmic perspective. Imagine the entire universe, with galaxies, nebulas and all. Zoom down to our galaxy, the Milky Way, and go on down to our own solar system. Imagine the Earth, your country and finally yourself standing right in the middle of the mess. Then you can laugh!

🔥

Gallows humor is a fantastic tool for turning a painful situation into something a little more positive. If your life is in ruins, if you feel like a ragdoll in a storm, make fun of it. Laugh loudly at yourself and your situation. That which is painful is experienced less intensely if you do not take it so seriously. If you are feeling bad and in addition have a very serious attitude about it, you will identify more with your own pain. When you do this, the way out of the darkness is much heavier. You can make it easier to get rid of the pain by laughing at yourself and your own situation.

Research has shown that laughter has a positive effect on health and mood. Laughter triggers the production of serotonin and endorphins. We have much to gain from laughing more. It is not always easy if life looks more like a nightmare. But if you manage it, you will see that it is difficult or even impossible to think dark thoughts while laughing.

Find out what you think is funny, and seek it out as often as possible. There are many funny videos on YouTube, for example (search for "funny cats"). Choose comedies you find funny,[4] instead of thrillers and action films. You can sign up for a laughter course or laughter yoga. A good life rule is making sure to laugh heartily at least once a day.

You can also force yourself to laugh. Numerous research experiments have proven that forcing oneself to laugh for one minute results in significant mood improvement. Find a clock and force

---

4 In the book *Anatomy of an Illness,* Norman Cousins describes how he healed himself of a serious sickness with high doses of vitamin C and daily exposure to comedy films.

yourself to laugh out loud. Do so every day you are depressed. Often the forced laughter will turn into a natural laughing fit; the entire practice feels comical. It is even more effective to do this together with a friend or family member; everything then becomes more humorous, and it becomes easier to switch over to natural laughter.

Play

During the course of growing up, many people stop playing. This is very unfortunate as there is much pleasure in play – much laughter and production of the important signal substances such as endorphins. Different games are suited for different phases of life, but to dare to play again we need to leave shame behind and rid ourselves of the meaningless thought of *now I am an adult, so playtime is over.*

People have a need to play, but society's norms keep us on a leash. One can get away from this societal pressure when together with children. Playing with children is legitimate behavior. Even better is to set up the game in a manner you find fun yourself. My own father was a master at this. Children were the best thing he knew, because he could play as much as he wanted without anybody else taking note of it.

If you do not have any children in your circle, you will need to think differently. Find adults who are still playful. As you play together you will find that others around you will also want to join in. There are "cool" adult games which society has accepted. There is much play in sports, especially team sports. Video games are play, and there are social video games as well. In our circle of friends, we have arranged paintball trips and produced films. Find out what you like to do, and do it! There are public groups for nearly all activities and hobbies you can think of. If you do not know many playful people, you can find them by joining such a group.

Music

Music is a powerful creator of atmosphere, and music that moves you can change your feelings directly. By listening to uplifting and energetic music on relatively high volume (watch your hearing), you can reduce negative and increase positive feelings. If you need to get something out, put on sad music. These things are somewhat obvious, but I do not believe everyone utilizes these tricks consciously. Many do quite the opposite: listen to sad music when they are already depressed when what they need is to lift the mood.

A group of friends once taught me a useful term: *angry music*. "Killing in the name of" by Rage against the Machine is an example of an angry song. If you feel like you are stuck in life, that you cannot move on due to one or several barriers, you can do the following: Find yourself some angry music you like, or music you dislike that is really angry and that you can pretend to like. Play the music loud. Stand right in front of the speakers and let the music make you angry. Imagine that you are exploding through all your problems.

Sometimes this practice will make it easier for you to identify what it is that is holding you back from moving forward. Maybe it is a person. If so, perhaps it is time for a break from this person. Maybe it is your job? Look for a new one. Ride on the wave of useful rage, and use it to break through whatever it is that is stopping you from getting to where you want to be. Reach a saturation point of frustration over your own demons and bad habits and use this to eliminate or change them.

To make music is even more powerful than to listen to it. If you do not already know how, learn to play the guitar or piano. It is surprisingly simple – with just three chords on the guitar, you can play thousands of rock and pop songs. Alternatively, you can buy a drum and go out into the forest and bang away. Out there nobody can hear you.

To help you become more aware of the degree to which music affects your mood, I have put together suggested playlists with different themes such as sad, happy, angry, and so on. These can be found on the website *kristianhall.com*. You can experiment with them and your own playlists until you have a better idea of just how music affects you.

𖠋

By singing and dancing for fifteen minutes each day you may become noticeably happier. These activities release endorphins and serotonin, substances which lead to increased feelings of happiness. In addition, you will reduce stress levels, increase blood circulation and reduce pain.

In many cultures we find a certain fear of attention, and this is probably the reason many people avoid singing and dancing. This fear has, over time, made singing and dancing something negative; we associate it with something embarrassing. The answer to this problem is simple: be alone!

The dance experiment

Choose a time when you are alone, and put on energetic music you like. Turn up the volume. Then begin to dance, slowly to begin with and then more wildly as time goes on. Keep it up for at least 10 minutes, and continue even if you feel silly. There comes a point when you stop feeling silly and begin to enjoy dancing. Continue until you reach this point. Let go of all your thoughts and judgments about dancing, and just throw yourself into the music.

Try this experiment before you go out and meet people, before you go to work, or when you are feeling down. Notice how your energy level rises dramatically. Do this every day for a week.

Song experiment

In this experiment there are some rules: To begin with it may be a good idea to be alone, for the first few times in any case. Next you must know the words to the song you will sing, or perhaps get the lyrics on paper or screen. Choose a song you like and that is relatively easy to sing. What I used to sing were various pop songs performed by the British artist Roger Whittaker, such as "Morning has broken".

Whether you want to sing with or without music in the background is up to you. For me it works best to sing to music. An advantage with this is that you sing together with the vocalist – you are not completely alone, so it is not so embarrassing. The third rule: You must sing loudly! You must really dig deep into your gut, let out a lot of air in the tones. As with dancing, do this every day for a week. It can be advantageous to choose two separate weeks so that it is easier to find out which of these two techniques has the greatest effect on you.

If you find that you enjoy singing, turn it into a hobby. Take singing classes or join a choir. You will be killing two birds with one stone: Doing something you enjoy, while doing something social.

Choose impulses wisely

If one has a dark and miserable mind, one is often drawn by dark things, surroundings and people. This is one of the demons' self-preservation mechanisms. They try to keep you unhappy by getting you to choose impulses that keep you down.

By reading newspapers or watching the evening news you can get the impression that the world is a dangerous place where murder and massacres occur everywhere, all the time. This is not the case at all. The world, aside from war and catastrophe zones, is largely made up of day-to-day happenings where most people wish each other well.

Filling your head with murder, rape and traffic accidents will certainly not improve your mood. As an experiment, you can shut out the news for a week. Watch the effect it has on you.

This principle also applies to books, films and other forms of media. When I was 18-19 years old, I read a lot of classical literature. It was primarily the dark authors who drew me. I read books like the *Journey to the End of the Night* by Louis-Ferdinand Céline and *The Book of Disquiet* by Fernando Pessoa. These two books (and others) pushed me deeper into depression. There are books and films that can take you so far down that it becomes quite hard to get back up again.

You can turn this effect on its head so that it works for you. You can become aware of how you are affected by different books and films, and use this to make you happier.

Try this experiment: Over the next month, only choose cultural impulses that improve your mood. Choose books and films that make you laugh and smile. You can get recommendations from the library or the local video store (the few that are left) or search online. Make a goal to see ten positive films and read three positive books next month.

Positive psychology

Positive psychology is an emerging field that is turning classical psychology upside down. Traditionally, psychology has focused on people's mental illnesses and what causes them. Positive psychology, however, is primarily concerned with activities and techniques which lead to a better overall mood.

Research on positive psychology has found that it has very good results with regard to reducing depression. This is one of the reasons I recommend that you find a psychologist who uses this method, preferably in combination with cognitive behavioral therapy. As I see it, this is the optimal therapy combination; you receive a direct improvement in how you feel, while working long-term to eliminate the negative thought patterns.

Whether you go to therapy or not, you can use the practices below, which are either formally a part of positive therapy or are closely related to it.

A practice with a white paper

Take a sheet of paper and draw a horizontal line across the middle. On the top write all of the things you can think of which make you happy, which you enjoy, or which you love to do such as skiing, being together with animals or children or playing the guitar. You can also write down the names of specific people who make you happy or who give you energy. Fill the page with as much as you can; if you run out of space you can continue the exercise on another sheet.

When you run out of things to write above the line, you then write down all the negative things in your life. Below the line write down all the things that drain your energy, that you dislike, or that make you depressed. Also write down the names of all the people who drain you or pull you down. Make sure that nobody sees the page.

Think through how your life looks right now – how much time you spend on the "bottom-half" and on the "top-half". Try to put a number to this. If you are in rough shape, perhaps you are 80 percent on the bottom and just 20 percent on the top. Note down this number and the date you performed the exercise.

The purpose of this exercise is twofold: First, it will give you a better awareness of how you live your life, and what triggers different feelings. Secondly, the exercise will provide you with a compass of sorts, something to steer by. Make yourself a promise that over the next week you will put aside more time, awareness and energy to the top half of the page at the cost of that which you wrote on the bottom half.

Over the course of the week you should keep the list in mind (or in your pocket) and actively choose the top half over the bottom half. If you feel the depression, tiredness or sadness coming on, take out the paper and choose an activity from the top.

When the week is over you can continue the exercise, or maybe make it a habit for life. Eventually you will not need to have the list in your pocket; you will automatically seek those activities which increase life-quality.

After a while, say half a year, you can compare the percentages from before and after you began the experiment. I believe you will be surprised at the result. Such things have a tendency to become positively addictive.

Gratitude journal

If I were to point out just one simple habit that reduces depression it would be thankfulness. Expressing thankfulness several times each day, for small things and large, is perhaps the most important thing depressed people can focus on improving. If you manage to go from thinking about what you lack to feeling real thankfulness for what you actually have, you have reached an important milestone in the process of getting rid of depression. As the self-hypnosis guru Adam Eason describes it, "If you only have a few dollars, be thankful for those you have."

An effective way of becoming more thankful is by keeping a gratitude diary. A gratitude diary is a notebook where you regularly, preferably daily, write down the things that you are thankful for.

> *To express thankfulness often is one of the most important means of overcoming depression.*

Buy a notebook, or use your diary. Note the day's date. Afterwards, write down at least three things that you are thankful for today. It can be anything from tiny to large and important things. It can be the fact that the sun is shining today, or the love you feel for somebody close to you. A good time to do this exercise is each evening before you go to bed. It feels good to go to bed with a feeling of thankfulness, and it will make it easier for you to sleep.

Do this every day for two weeks. Observe any changes in your mental state. Even if the effect in your case is small, I would encourage you to continue the exercise throughout those two weeks. Research has found that depressed people experience a considerable mood improvement when they use such a diary.

&

For my part, I say a loud inner *Thanks!* each time I experience something positive, both small things and large. I say *Thanks!* if I run for the bus and it waits for me, if I see something funny on the street, if a stranger smiles at me, if I eat something delicious, if the sun shines, if I see something beautiful in nature, and so on and so on. You get the point. This little habit can really revolutionize your life!

What went well today?

This technique is somewhat similar to the gratitude diary. You can choose one of them, or you can do both. Doing both will increase the effect. On the other hand, if you were to do all of the techniques in this book daily, you would need several hours each day. This is not realistic, but you can choose your favorites and concentrate on them.

Over the next week you will try to do the following each evening before you go to bed: Take out a notebook or diary (you can also do this digitally). Write down three things which went well today, and why they went well.

For example, you could write: I took a long walk today, and it felt good. As to the 'cause' you can write: I have gotten better at exercising and train daily because I have decided to improve my life.

Another example may be: I prepared a concise and informative presentation at work today. The cause in this case may be: I had conducted good research.

Another example: I woke up before 10 o'clock today. Cause: I decided to do so last night, as sleeping in does not help me, and it is better to get up.

Do not drop the cause when you do this exercise. By writing down the cause to the thing which went well, over time you will see that you do more which is positive than you may think. You have much more control over your own behavior and life than you may be aware of.

After a week you will know how well this technique works for you. If it works, simply continue. Make it a habit.

Find the positive in the suffering

One metaphor I like is that the human mind is like a square room. The people in the middle of the room are unaware that there is an outside. But in reality there is a whole world out there, with weird animals and monsters and wild landscapes.

Then something dramatic happens to the people in the room. A life-crisis, a loss or anxiety and depression. It can also be something positive, such as the birth of a child.

In the metaphor, the dramatic event arrives as a giant who enters the room. He is carrying a sledgehammer and bangs down one of the walls. Behind the wall, the people see all of the monsters and demons, but also the beautiful landscapes. The people have become one experience richer, even if the experience may have been traumatic and frightening.

Each dramatic experience will change you as a person, sometimes for the worse. But even terrible experiences or life crises can bring about something positive. For example, life crises make you into a better conversational partner, into a more interesting and nuanced person. Your own suffering will make it easier for you to help others in similar situations.

Look at the great artists or musicians in the world. Who among them had/have a simple emotional life? If you are struggling, is it possible to use your suffering to create something beautiful? But do not make your suffering into your identity; do not romanticize it.

Losing Dad tightened the bonds between my mother, sister and me. Our survival strategy was to talk a lot about the loss and how we missed him. This has led to an improvement in our communication. It has made us wiser, even something as horrible as losing a dear family member can have positive sides.

If you manage to get through the crisis in somewhat good shape, you will have grown as a person – now you know of one more thing that you can handle. The next crisis will seem less frightening because you know that you have been through the flames before. Each time I meet opposition in life now, I think that it will take a lot to match the hell I have experienced and survived before. It has made me into a rather strong person.

It is my opinion that life becomes richer when one continually tears down the walls of the room in which they stand, even if the walls are hiding demons and nightmares. For me, it is better to live a life that is exciting and sometimes painful than one that drones along in safety and boredom.

Try to find pride (and still humility) in the fact that you have stood in the fire. Pride and understanding. Understanding you can later use to help others. Life is both parts, both pain and happiness.

Reframing

Reframing is a potent tool which can seem difficult for depressed people in the beginning, but can be incorporated as a new habit in the same way as when you learn other things in life (through repetition).

Reframing refers to seeing a life situation in a new light, whereby one focuses their attention on the positive. In many situations this may be difficult, sometimes impossible, such as when someone dies. This is rarely positive. But fortunately life is primarily made up of completely day-to-day things which we can choose ourselves how we want to interact.

Let me give a few examples from my own life: My hair is becoming thinner. One day it will be so thin that I have three choices: I can do a comb-over, I can get a hair transplant, or I can shave my head. When I reach the point that I am no longer particularly handsome with thin, fluffy hair, I will choose the last option. So when I think about the future of my hair, I can either get bummed out or I can think that I will save a lot of money at the barber. It is obvious which way of thinking will help the most. That is why I chose it.

Another example is that I, during military service twenty years ago, developed chronic tinnitus. I can choose to think about the sound and that absolute silence will never again exist for me. Or I can think that tinnitus was a significant hurdle which I managed to overcome, and that tinnitus gave me a useful experience in controlling my thoughts and pushing away the sound as though it did not exist. And now I can use the same technique to push away or tone down other sufferings, by simply not focusing my attention on them.

Each time something happens to you that previously made you down or depressed, force yourself to find at least one positive thing in it. If it feels ridiculous and forced, search with all you have for something positive and hold onto it. When you succeed, note it down in your diary or commit it to memory. Over time you will have more and more successes, and this ability will eventually become a new habit.

Put others first

If you want quick results in the quest for a better life, put others first! There is a lot of research regarding how doing something for others affects the mood, and the results indicate rather unanimously that doing good deeds has a significant positive effect.

I believe that all people become happier by being kind and that maybe this is the greatest reason why we should be this way. I do not believe in pure altruism. But I think altruism feels fantastic! There is also evidence for this from research. Helping others is one of the surest and fastest means of getting in a better mood. For more information about this (and positive psychology in general), read *Flourish* by Martin Seligman.

If you are one of those who find it easier to help others than to receive help yourself, maybe you can think that helping *you* is pleasurable for the one offering help. It would be a good deed to let your helpers help you.

Why we get happy by being kind is a question with many answers. The one I prefer is that evolution has over several millennia programmed us to be rewarded for taking care of others. This was a clear advantage for the tribe – we are stronger together. For me, it is more important that we are all connected on many levels. At the core we are all a part of the same whole.

Helping others puts in motion a positive spiral. You put others first, you make others happy, you become happy, you are motivated to continue doing this. Then others around you begin to do the same. You have initiated a chain reaction, a three-dimensional wave of good which propagates from you. This wave can travel far, and your little effort in the beginning can lead to unimaginable positive results for other people.

Another good reason for doing something for others is that you transfer your attention away from yourself and your own suffering. Much of the reason you feel bad is because you go around thinking about your own feelings and pain all the time. If you think about what you can do for those around you, you will automatically think less about your own suffering and this will reduce the pain you are experiencing. This is related to focusing your attention on that which you are thankful for. It is obvious that one can get depressed by over-focusing on the negative. To improve you must redirect this, even if it means forcing yourself in the beginning.

Another technique is to find an original way to help others, something you have never done before. If you do not have any good ideas, the Red Cross may be a good place to start. They arrange volunteer programs where you can, for example, help children with their homework or visit the elderly.

❧

One time when I took the subway, somebody had hung up a note at the station. It read as follows:

> *Try not to backtalk anybody today.*
> *Try not to backtalk anybody for three days.*
> *Try not to backtalk anybody for three weeks.*
> *Try not to backtalk anybody for a year.*
> *See what happens to your life.*

May this challenge carry on.

Forgiveness

At times in my life I have looked down on Christianity's teachings on forgiveness. I saw forgiveness as weak, unfair and unrealistic. People who hurt others do not deserve forgiveness, I thought. They deserve punishment.

It was relatively recently that I realized Christianity is right with regard to forgiveness. You do not need to turn the other cheek out of consideration for the one who hurt you. You do it for yourself. Too many of us go around feeling victimized, filled with bitterness and self-pity. We feel sorry for ourselves because someone has hurt us. We use much time, attention and energy on hate and anger against those who have bruised or battered us.

Forgiveness stops this process. You can literally overnight begin to empty your burden of suffering which you have carried every day, by simply forgiving those who hurt you. It requires courage, but if you are willing to forgive you will feel an enormous relief because you have released yourself from the person who has hurt you and from the painful memories.

You do not need to meet the person who hurt you to forgive him or her. It is enough to simply decide to strike out that part of your life: *After this moment I will never again entertain feelings*

for the person who hurt me. I will simply forgive and refuse to
spend time, attention or energy on that person again.

❧

Here is another technique for reducing hate, a technique which
originates from Buddhism. It is a radical technique which will
not work for everyone, but one with which I have personally had
much success. I imagine that this technique may be too extreme
in cases where someone has seriously injured you. But you have
nothing to lose; if it does not work, simply quit the exercise.

Each time you feel yourself beginning to hate the person
or group you hate, send love or well-wishes in their direction
instead! This will feel strange at first, but eventually you will
understand why this works in practice. It feels liberating to send
love to someone or something you have previously hated. It feels
as though you have reversed the flow of energy, from an invading
negative stream from the object of hate, to a positive energy
stream from you. In a sense, you push the object of hate farther
away from you, and this is exactly what you want to achieve.

Devote your life to something larger than yourself

The British researcher and inventor Buckminster Fuller experienced a period of depression in his youth. He was on the brink
of suicide. Instead of taking his own life, he decided to give it
away – to humanity. He decided to dedicate his life to research
which would be his gift to humanity. The result of this is well
summarized in his autobiography *Critical Path*.

Another example of the same phenomenon is the Norwegian
Ada Sofie Austegard, who lost her daughter in a terrible way. Her
eight-year-old daughter was raped and murdered in a criminal
case which has etched itself into the Norwegian psyche because
the crimes were so incredibly gruesome. How can one go on in

life after losing a child in such a way? One way is to dedicate your life to something greater than yourself. That was exactly what Austegard did when she founded a foundation in the name of her daughter, an organization which works to prevent assaults on children.

You can do something similar. If your life today is so painful that you are considering terminating it, you can give it away instead. You can dedicate your life to one or more causes which are larger than yourself. Monasteries across the world are filled with people who have made this choice.

Of course, you do not need to join a monastery. You can choose a cause you care about, such as climate change or global poverty. You can found your own organization to help individuals in your area. You can engage in religious organizations which you hold close. There are thousands of good causes and people who need your help.

Exercise and Fitness

Exercise and fitness have numerous positive effects: more energy; better mood, more self-confidence, increased concentration, better health, better sleep, pain reduction and increased willpower. In the context of this book, increased self-confidence is one of the most important effects, along with direct improvements in mood. Lack of self-confidence is often a contributing cause to depression. Self-confidence is ammunition in the battle against your demons.

Many struggle with training as often as they would like, or as often as their body and mind would benefit from. It is normal to start an exercise program, only to quit after a few weeks. Often people set their targets too high and then beat themselves up over being "lazy" if they do not manage to meet them. The first days and weeks of exercise can be physically uncomfortable if you are starting from a low activity level. Maybe your muscles and tendons hurt; maybe you feel ill or out of breath.

The answer to all of this is to begin by setting small goals. You can begin by walking for 10 minutes each day. If you take the bus you can hop off one stop before or after your destination. If you live near the forest (or other places of nature), take your walk there to combine exercise and contact with nature. Perhaps turn on some uplifting music while you walk.

In Japan people operate with a concept they call *shinrin-yoku*, which can be translated to "forest bathing." In my home country, Norway, there is a tradition of walking in the forest and mountains, something Norwegians have done for hundreds of years. In Japan this is being researched, and the results are fascinating.

Being in a forest (and nature in general) lowers the pulse and blood pressure, as well as reducing stress hormones, while heart rate variability increases. Heart rate variability is a metric which tells you about your stress level. The higher the heart rate variability is, the lower the stress level. That bill lying in a drawer, the one which you do not have the money to pay, is not quite as worrisome when you are out on a stroll.

Research shows that taking a so-called "green break," a walk or a stop in a green area, leads to increased willpower. We get a cartload of small gifts when we take a walk in nature. We can take advantage of this in order to improve our health and mood.

Some of the worst thoughts you can think are those that arise when you are lying sleepless in a dark room. Some of the best thoughts are those experienced while walking. Being in motion allows you to experience a dynamic world around you; this has a tendency to affect the way you think. Repetitive, painful thoughts can be released by dynamic thinking that points the way out of an impasse. This is often my experience.

Another important principle is to train in a way which you find fun. For many of us, lifting weights or running on a treadmill is not especially motivating. There are many ways to exercise in a way which is more enjoyable. Many of them have the added advantage of including other people, and thereby combine the need for exercise with the need for meeting friends or making new ones. Most team sports have this. Other examples are dancing, martial arts and rock climbing. There are hundreds of activities which will give you both regular contact with other people and the exercise you need.

It is not important what you do, only that you move. Preferably you should be active three times each week, and it is sufficient to simply walk fast enough to increase your heart rate and maybe work up a sweat. Sweat helps to eliminate waste from your body, waste which can interfere with your body and mind working optimally.

A motivational trick often used with children and that also works well for adults is a "star calendar." Buy a calendar and some stickers – stars, circles or hearts. Each time you exercise or train put a sticker on that day on the calendar. This can be done for other things as well, like days without sweets or cigarettes. When you have a certain amount of stickers, give yourself a reward: Go out for dinner, or buy yourself something you have been wanting. Alternatively, you can use electronic aids, such as the app Coach.me (referred to earlier).

We can also say it like the training expert Yngvar Andersen: *Forget motivation*! His point is that we can choose to make exercise into something we simply must do, regardless of whether we think it is boring or uncomfortable.

If you are suffering from physical ailments which stop you from exercising, tai chi or yoga may be an option for you. In addition to exercise, these forms of training will lead to improved moods and mental states. Tai chi and yoga are physical meditation techniques. These body exercises can be modified in such a manner that they can be done by absolutely anyone (pregnant, elderly etc.). They can be used as a part of a rehabilitation program following an injury. You can buy an instruction book or DVD, or search online for a course in your area.

◊

People have a biological need for sunlight. Your skin requires it in order to produce vitamin D (low vitamin D levels are connected to depression). In addition, we have a strong psychological need for it; research has found that exposure to sunlight leads to the production of endorphins. It is well-known that northerly inhabitants can get light depression during the darkness of winter.

Sunlight is a powerful source of energy. Ensure that you get a daily dose of sunlight if you can. If you live in the north, you can take a trip south during winter, if you are able.

The combination of sun and sea, or sun and air, is even more effective. Standing a few minutes along a south-facing coast and "bathing" in the sun and sea can feel like a religious experience. The same applies to a hike in an open landscape, where the empty space filled with air encompasses you.

Diet

I am convinced that in ten years time the world's doctors will stress the importance of a healthy diet to a greater degree than they do today. My view of illness is that a combination of prolonged stress and poor diet are largely to blame (here I am referring to somatic illnesses; depression generally has other causes), even if some people are simply unlucky and others are genetically predisposed to certain illnesses. Food can be medicine, and I eagerly await the blooming of this new paradigm.

In addition to preventing and curing illnesses, you can also improve your mood and quality of life by changing diet. How many people do you know who get grumpy and irritated by low blood sugar? Maybe you belong to this group yourself. I certainly do.

I remember what the hours after 5 p.m. were like at home before my wife and I discovered this. We came home from work, grumpy as a storm, and began arguing about things like dirty dishes or cooking simply because our blood sugar levels were too low.

This is easy to do something about. Perhaps one of the simplest tricks is to buy a bag of nuts or beef jerky that you can keep at work or school, and eat a handful before going home. Many people eat chocolate around 4-5 p.m., but this is a bad choice as it leads to a peak in blood sugar which soon turns to a dramatic drop, as insulin is produced to remove the glucose from the blood. The sudden drop in blood sugar will leave you tired and in a bad mood.

I would strongly advise changing your diet to reduce your intake of sugar (though you may indulge yourself from time to time) and eating as much healthy food as possible which releases energy more slowly. In professional jargon this is known as glycemic index (GI) and glycemic load (GL), and there are many books written on the subject. You do not need to buy a book; you can look up a list of GL in food online, and eat foods which have the lowest GL. GL is a better measurement than GI as the former also takes into consideration how many calories (energy) are found in the product. For example, a watermelon has a high GI but a somewhat low GL, as it is a relatively calorie-poor fruit. In other words, you can eat watermelon with a clear conscience despite its high GI.

I believe it is wise to change diet gradually instead of revolutionizing it overnight. The first step can be to acquire supplements that include all of the vitamins and minerals the body needs, as well as a pack of high-quality Omega-3. Later, you can reduce your intake, little by little, of pre-made meals and food which is high in fat and sugar. At the same time, you can phase in fruit and vegetables and replace a portion of your meat intake with lentils and beans.

A good way to start is to begin the day with a smoothie made from berries and bananas. Buy a blender and mix frozen berries, bananas and yogurt or a dairy substitute. It tastes good and gives the body the important nutrients it needs to promote a positive mood.

Here is a recipe: Mix a handful of frozen spinach with a handful of frozen broccoli. Add two bananas. Then pour in equal parts of pineapple juice and dairy substitute (e.g., almond or oatmeal milk) until you have the desired smoothie consistency. If you have some, add plant-based Omega 3-6-9 oil and a little coconut oil. Mix it in the blender. Spinach and broccoli smoothies may sound pretty gross, but they taste surprisingly good. Spinach and broccoli are among the healthiest vegetables out there, and this an easy way to consume a lot of them.

Surround yourself with people who uplift you

Human relationships are among the most important sources of happiness in life. But this is unfortunately not the case for everyone – at least, not all the time. There are people who hold other people down, sometimes intentionally, and it can be important to isolate yourself from such people. If you are depressed it is important to clean up your relationships, to create distance from those who bring you down and to give priority those who lift you up.

Focus your attention on the best people you have around you – the gold mines: those who are there for you when you need them, those who give you energy and good feelings. The exercise "practice with a white paper", described earlier will have shown you who they are. Prioritize spending time with these people.

A good indicator of a relationship's quality is whether the person in question gives you energy or takes it from you. If you are tired or bored each time you meet a person, it can be time to reconsider this relationship. By this I do not necessarily mean that you should leave this person for good. Perhaps the person in question is going through a tough phase in life as well. Maybe this person needs help, and maybe you can provide it. Going through a crisis together with another person will deepen the relationship.

Patience and tolerance are important virtues when relating to other people. We can tolerate when others are out of line from time to time. What should not be tolerated, however, is if another person continually treats us poorly or drains our energy. Pull yourself slowly away from such people; they are not worth your time, and they can act as barriers to your self-improvement.

Some people can and should be avoided altogether. There are people who intentionally push down those around them, for example, by using damaging language like "you are so fat," or "you'll never succeed with anything." In some cases, they may do this to gain a psychological advantage over you, so that it is easier for them to manipulate and control you. These people are like poison to those around them.

&

Some are so fortunate as to grow up in functional families, where family members care about each other, support one another and provide reciprocal happiness and comfort. This is generally not the case for those who come from so-called dysfunctional families. These are families where one or more parents suffer from alcoholism or another type of addiction, or have different degrees of mental illness, or where physical or mental assault occurs.

I have seen research suggesting that nearly half of the families in the USA are labeled as dysfunctional. Considering this, it's not surprising that so many people suffer from depression and other mental illness.

Some families are like black holes. Because the parents have mental and emotional baggage, they end up transferring their own problems to their children. One can end up in a situation where most members of the family have some form of emotional problem, and often share the same problems.

If you come from such a family, it is important to liberate yourself from it. The best scenario is when you can spend time with your family without it leading to a worsening of your mood. In many cases this can be difficult, and it may be necessary to isolate yourself physically from family members.

Where you may be standing now, in the initial phase of a process to improve yourself and your own life, you are likely vulnerable. At this point it does not take more than one negative comment by a careless friend or family member for you to lose heart and slide back down to where you started. An example may be: "Are *you* into that self-help crap too?" It is especially in this phase that you must protect yourself from negative family members and friends.

After a while you will become more able to face those who would hold you down in the mud, where they may themselves reside. When you have built up your own strength, you will not have problems being with negative people; when they come, you can simply mentally shrug your shoulders to negative comments and let them bounce off you.

You do not need to cut ties with anyone on a permanent basis, only reduce the contact with the most negative people when you are vulnerable. Spend less time with your family in this phase; try to especially avoid familiar situations which you know can set you back emotionally. If you are going to study, enroll in school in another town. If you are an adult, move farther away from those you need to distance yourself from, or simply choose to spend less time with them.

🔥

Behavioral patterns can be inherited. Those who grow up in a dysfunctional family can end up forming a dysfunctional family of their own. Children who grow up with alcoholic parents are more likely to become alcoholics themselves, or find themselves an alcoholic partner. Children who are abused at home will on average beat their child more often than those who were not. I call this phenomenon *the dark chain*.

Inheritance of negative behavioral patterns can occur over many generations. This is why it is important that somebody says, "Enough is enough!" and stops the dark chain. This can provide an additional motivation for people suffering from depression or other mental illnesses. If you come from such a dysfunctional family, make a choice where you decide it stops with you. Whatever your father or mother (or both) struggled with, you will fight within yourself and not pass it on to your own children.

The Super Week

Now I will compile several of the techniques provided thus far in the book and squeeze them into one week. Every day of the week, do the following:

- Completely avoid the news in newspapers, online and on TV.
- Exercise for at least 15 minutes.
- Avoid sweets altogether, or at least reduce your intake dramatically.
- Eat as healthily as possible.
- Eliminate or cut down on your intake of alcohol and other drugs.
- Go to bed at a time which allows for eight hours of sleep.
- Do at least one good deed.
- Say "Thanks!" to yourself each time you experience something positive.
- Write a little in your journal. Reflect upon how you are feeling, but focus on which exercises you are doing and the effect they have on you.
- Jot down in your journal things that you are thankful for.

In addition, you have the following tasks this week:

- Begin the day by singing or dancing for 15 minutes in the morning (sing and dance every other day).
- Watch at least three positive movies, and read at least one positive novel.

- Try to avoid the people who bring you down, and spend lots of time with those who uplift you and make you happy.
- Avoid beating yourself up over not completing parts of the list above.

PART 3

DEPRESSION'S COMPANIONS

Related conditions

As a rule, depression does not come alone. It often operates together with other problems and disorders. Depression can be triggered by such things as grief, loneliness and anxiety. It can also trigger secondary problems such as shame, bitterness and guilt. What comes first is not really important. In this part of the book I write about how you can manage these related conditions. Here you can choose the chapters which are relevant to you and ignore those which are not.

Worries and sleeplessness

Some people are worried about everything all of the time, while others have not a worry in the world. For many people with depression, worries are part of their everyday life. You may worry about your own sickness, about those close to you and about the future. Fortunately, there are effective techniques to reduce worries.

One technique is to use your journal to write down your worries. This alone will reduce the intensity. Let us say that you are worried about a project at work. You write about the project and what you are worried about. In so doing you illuminate the project from different perspectives and minimize the risk that you have forgotten something (which is often the source of the worry). When you are finished writing about the worry, you will often find that the risk for the undesired event is much smaller than you believed, or that you have already done what you could to reduce the consequences of whatever you are worried about.

Another technique is to write down all the things you are worried about on small notes and place these pages in a drawer or a box. Make this a habit. At regular intervals, say every six months, you empty the box and read all of the notes. You will see that there are very few of these worries which actually became a reality. Reflect on this and remember it the next time you are worried about something.

Living in the here and now effectively reduces worries. The worries disappear like mist before the sun when you are able to live in the moment. The reason is that the brain is only able to process

97

one dominant thought at a time (try worrying while solving a complex math problem). If your brain is completely occupied with registering the details of your immediate surroundings, it will not have the capacity to obsess over worries.

Let us try it one more time. Use your surroundings as a bridge away from your worries. Start by looking around you and use a little time to observe your surroundings with as many senses as possible. Take note of the colors and textures of things around you. Listen to which sounds surround you; try to take in the smells. Then gradually turn your attention inward, toward how you breathe, how your body feels, where you ache, to what degree you are relaxed. Move a finger over the skin of your arm and be aware of how the nerve signals are registered. Do not analyze the feelings; just register them without dwelling on them.

The worries disappeared, right? Perhaps for no longer than a second, but they disappeared completely. Now you have done this exercise twice, and you have gained a powerful tool to spend less time on your daily worries. Each time they arise you can do this exercise and have a mental recess. The fact that you have taught yourself this is in itself worry-reducing – now you know that you have a secret weapon to be used when needed.

Do this exercise every day for two weeks, and eventually try to do the same when you do the dishes, while you are at work, when you go to bed and so on. Focus your entire attention on what you are doing, at all times.

Both depression and worries are connected to sleeplessness. These are problems which are mutually reinforcing. For example: You are worried about your job performance and this is affecting your sleep. When you sleep poorly, you perform less well at work and the worry increases. Write down your worries, and you will sleep better.

Many people who cannot sleep struggle with it because they think too much. They lie for hours and torture themselves with thoughts like: *If I don't sleep now, tomorrow will be a catastrophe!* Is it strange it is hard to sleep, then?

Many people I know have found cognitive behavioral therapy helpful as it is directed toward breaking habitual thinking patterns like *I definitely won't get any sleep tonight!* My wife had one session using cognitive behavioral therapy after months of bad sleep. The therapist asked her quite simply, "If none of the techniques you have tried to sleep work, why can't you just admit that this is something you have no control over?" The following night she fell asleep immediately. For me, this story is an example of how demons (such as sleeplessness) sometimes can be defeated by very simple steps.

My own method of defeating sleeplessness was somewhat different. I once received a top grade in an exam after sleeping less than an hour the night before. This became proof – a symbol – that it is possible to function in spite of a bad night's sleep. After this, I always think, *I can't sleep, but it doesn't matter. It is nice lying here anyway.* Usually I fall asleep shortly after.

The best way to defeat sleeplessness is to stop worrying about it. This may sound quite simple, but if you stop caring about whether or not you sleep, the problem will often take care of itself. Think: *If I can't sleep tonight, there's always tomorrow night.* Or: *If I don't sleep now, I will get up and read my book.* Or: *It's fine if I don't sleep, because it is so comfortable to lie here and relax.*

Meditation is another effective tool against sleeplessness. Later in the book you will find a meditation method which is ideal for this.

Anxiety

Anxiety can be a serious psychological illness, which can come in thousands of different forms and degrees. It can be difficult to find a quick fix to get rid of anxiety and it may be necessary to seek out professional help. Cognitive behavioral therapy has also been demonstrated to be effective against anxiety.

As with depression, it is important to get an overview of what makes you anxious, and to then systematically and decisively avoid these triggering factors. If the anxiety is directed toward something specific, as is the case with regard to social anxiety for example, gradual exposure will also be an important part of your healing. A therapist can help you with this.

For those with acute anxiety, their entire world falls apart. The world is experienced as a nightmare which has become a reality. Everything is frightening. The most important thing for a person experiencing acute anxiety is to seek out company. Try to avoid being alone, especially at night. If the anxiety attack lasts for days, move in with a good friend or a family member, somebody you trust, who can help you take the sting out of the attack. Talk about the anxiety; putting into words what you experience may reduce the intensity and make the experience less frightening. A journal can be useful here. Write down what you experience and any reflections you may have on the anxiety.

When you suffer from acute anxiety it is important to regain control. Do not try to grasp your entire life, as this will be too large a task if you feel that you are "hanging in thin air." Concentrate instead on smaller pieces of the day. Here is a concrete technique to this end:

The technique is concerned with getting through the day by *breaking it up into very small portions.* Special Forces soldiers train in such mental techniques to be used when they are on missions which include a very high level of stress, such as when they are behind enemy lines. They are trained to focus their attention toward one thing at a time and to complete these small tasks without thinking about the terrifying totality.

Say to yourself, "I am [your name], and now I will eat breakfast." Next, concentrate only on eating breakfast. Turn this into a game by seeing to what degree you can focus on your breakfast, on what you are eating, on how it tastes, on how it feels in your mouth, on the sounds around you. Fifteen minutes later say, "I am [your name], and now I will take a shower." Take a shower as though for the first time – enjoy how the warm water relaxes your muscles, how the water runs down your body; try to take in how the soap smells, how the drops on the shower cabinet are running down the Plexiglas.

Concentrate on one small task at a time. Try to take in every detail of everything you do; use all of your senses. Do this until the anxiety attack passes and you can take control of your life again.

Grief

Grief comes in as many forms as there are people grieving. Some may have lost a close family member without feeling much at all, while a child who loses their cat can be completely crushed.

The process of coming out of grief is relatively simple, but brutal – you must accept the help of time. Time (partially) heals all wounds. Grief is the mind's natural way of managing a loss. It is a necessary process you must go through in order to adjust to a new situation – a situation where somebody or something is missing.

In the USA people are routinely given antidepressants for grief, even those suffering from broken hearts. I believe this to be unwise. There is a reason for the sorrow and melancholy you feel when grieving. There is nothing pathological about those feelings; they are not symptoms which one can or should cure. Time is the only true healer.

At the same time, it is important to clean up the mess of feelings which the bereaved often find themselves experiencing. One thing which makes grief complicated is that it is generally mixed with other feelings.

One example is guilt. Maybe you argued with the person who died just before he or she passed away. Maybe things were left unsaid. Here therapy can be most useful. A professional therapist is trained in how to braid together the many feelings and put things in their proper place. A good alternative to therapy is talking to a friend or relative who has experienced loss. Perhaps you can also seek out a grief support group.

Through the tough and prolonged work of sorting feelings, you will end up being left with just the grief. A "pure" grief is easier to handle than one which is mixed with other feelings. When you have removed the other elements, you can then focus your attention on the loss and to a greater degree relate passively to the grief. You can let go and simply let the current of your emotional river carry you downstream. Let the feelings take you where you need to be. Know that the painful feelings will lessen with time. This much is certain.

In the meantime it is important to learn the art of escape. This is not about a desperate escape without control, but instead a decision to take a break from the grief. Nobody can cry all of the time.

Do things that make you happy and that make time pass quickly. If you like movies, go to the theater frequently! Exercise, play video games or go to the museum. Do whatever you find to be the most distracting.

ه

A few years after I lost my dad I heard a story about a father who lost his son in an accident. The story tells of how the father simply could not bear to spend such a large part of his life grieving. He made a conscious choice and was able to hold off the grief each day. But he had a "box of grief" with photos and letters from his son which he brought out once a year, when he would then grieve with intensity.

For me, while in the middle of grieving for my dad, this was a provoking story. Choose to not grieve? It felt like choosing to forget him. Several years later I first understood that this can be a navigable path in many cases. However, it is probably not wise to do something like this in the early phases of grief.

But after a while you can make this choice. When it can happen is up to each individual, perhaps some years in the future. This is not about forgetting the person who is gone, but more about focusing attention toward all of the positive things he or she brought to your life. It is about choosing to meet the day with a positive attitude, pretending you are happy until you actually feel happy, instead of going through yet another day filled with sorrow, melancholy and maybe depression.

For me, when I realized that I could allow myself this, it played a part of my victory over depression. I thought about what Dad would have wanted for me. He would definitely not have wished for me to have suffered several more years with grief; he would have wanted me to be happy and to concentrate on life and the opportunities it presents. The vast majority of those who pass away would wish this for those they cared about.

Do not let too many years pass in grief; *grieve* until you have done away with the largest part of your grieving, and then make a conscious decision that enough is enough, and that now you will move on in life. Maybe you need a transition ritual to succeed with this. Such rituals are described later in the book.

Heartbreak

Heartbreaks are quite special cases; nobody has died. What you have lost, and what you are grieving, is a future together with the person you could not get, or the one you could no longer be together with. This does not necessarily make the grief less painful. My sister has told me that she has experienced heartbreak as intense as her grief over Dad. The good news is that heartbreaks, as a rule, are of a much shorter duration than grief following a death.

In cases of intense heartbreak, it may help to mentally cut the ties to the person you are no longer with (or never had). It may help to physically avoid the person. In extreme cases you can consider moving or changing workplaces if this is what is necessary to create distance. It will be much more difficult to get over the grief if you see the person regularly.

The same is true for all of the things and memories. All items that will remind you of the person you are heartbroken over must be removed. I would not recommend disposing of them – you may regret this later – but rid yourself of them by other means. You can, for example, deliver a photo album to a friend or family member to take care of until you have gotten over your grief. Delete emails and text messages from the person, or archive them on a removable hard drive which you can then put away if you do not want to erase them permanently. You can draw a line in your life, mark once and for all that the life you had with the person is over. This is best done with a transition ritual.

Bitterness and self-pity

The bitter find themselves at a dead end. In order to come out of bitterness, you must take a few steps backward before going forward again. Bitterness is closely related to self-pity, something which functions as a brake on the healing process. Self-pity can seem like a comfortable pillow to rest the head upon, a substitute for the closeness one maybe misses. This may be fine in acute situations; everybody needs something to lean on, and when all else fails, self-pity can be useful.

Self-pity is like giving yourself a sweaty hug. Sooner or later you must let go of self-pity in order to move on. It is you who decides when this will happen, but the sooner the better.

Bitterness is self-pity which has grown rancid – old, nasty self-pity. It would do you good to get rid of it, and one way of achieving this is by realizing how pathetic bitterness really is. It is a hard thing to realize and accept. What you are really doing is throwing away that which may be the only thing you have had to hold on to for some time, something which may have served as an important part of your identity while you have been depressed and unhappy.

Latch on to alternative foundations when you have decided to act on this: social network (friends and family), professional help (therapists, doctors, etc.) or open support groups. Or you can choose a cause larger than yourself, as described earlier in the book.

◊

Something which is closely related to bitterness is the idea that everything is meaningless (nihilism). I lived with this perspective for years. My life was meaningless, the world was meaningless – absolutely everything was meaningless.

But then I realized something important: If everything is meaningless, then you are actually free. If there are no rules or laws or values, then *you are free to make your own*, free to do whatever you want, and to make your own rules and laws. This is a fantastic foundation to build upon. But you must dare to put the bitterness behind you, dare to admit that life can be good, and that you appreciate an embrace from someone you care about.

Envy

Envy is bitterness' cousin. Many who are down are envious of those around them. They are envious of people in their own circle, of celebrities or their neighbor. When you hurt, it may be difficult to be happy for another's success. Perhaps you wish, to a degree, that others would even fail. Do not beat yourself up if this is true for you, as this is normal, and quite human.

Envy actually has a positive function. If you continually envy certain aspects of the lives of those around you, such as that they have children, that they have an apparently happy marriage, or other such things, you have received an important signal about what you most value in your own life. This is a signal about what is important to you, and at the same time about what you are lacking. You can use this to direct your own hunt for these elements.

At the same time envy must be taken seriously. If you are envious, this means that you focus too much attention toward others (and what you lack) and not enough toward yourself (and what you have). If you are envious, you are using time, energy and attention on comparing your status, your relationships and your financial situation to those of others.

I believe that we must get rid of envy to move on, to stop comparing ourselves to others and thereby using their lives as a yardstick for how good we have it in comparison. We should use *our own life* as a yardstick!

One problem which arises when using others' lives as yard-sticks is that you never know what their lives are actually like. You see the popular girl in school and think that her life must be perfect, or you see the neighbors' nice house and car and conclude that they are living the dream. But you can never know this. Material wealth rarely leads to actual happiness alone, as long as you are above a certain basic level. Lasting, real wellbeing is found in positive emotions (such as happiness and love), engagement, relationships, experienced purpose and mastery.

A good technique for reducing and eventually eliminating envy is to keep a gratitude journal, as described earlier. By keeping this journal, you move your attention from what you are lacking to what you have. By using the other techniques in this book, by improving yourself, you will gradually gain more to be thankful for. If you are sick or have few good relationships, it may be difficult to be thankful for anything. But what is important is that you begin somewhere, to force yourself to seek out the positive elements.

If you manage to take a step over this gulley, then you have taken a quantum leap in the direction of a better life. If you do not believe me, simply try this whole-heartedly for one week. Start each day by going through the things that you have in life, which in spite of everything, you are happy and thankful for.

Make yourself a promise right here and now: Gradually focus your attention less on your own suffering, on what you are lacking, on your envy of others, and instead to gradually focus your attention on what you actually have and be honestly thankful for this.

Regret, guilt and shame

The last thing I did before Dad died was lie to him. I was going to have some friends over for a parents-out-of-town party, but I told him something else before he left for the evening he never returned from. This is rather common behavior for a teenager, but the guilt hung over me for years.

During the course of life people will make innumerable mistakes and blunders. It is impossible to avoid mistakes, and they have an important function: They are our primary source of learning. People who manage to see mistakes as something positive are fortunate, they are able to learn from these errors and then move forward without shame or guilt.

This is something people with depression must learn. Shame and guilt follow depression and maintain it. People are ashamed for being sick or weak, because those around them see their weakness. People experience feelings of guilt, knowing that those close to them suffer when seeing their pain.

The trick is to give yourself greater leeway, to realize that you do not make more mistakes than others and that it is entirely okay to make mistakes. Talk about whatever you are ashamed of, perhaps with your therapist, so that you gain an external perspective on the situation. This will help you to see that there may be nothing to be ashamed of or to feel guilty about. You must forgive yourself, plain and simple.

To help yourself let go, you can tailor your own little ritual. You can write down on paper the situation that bothers you, which you then put in a carton box that you bury. Alternatively, you can burn the page or wrap it around something that floats (and that will dissolve itself over time) and throw it in the sea.

Suicidal thoughts

Sometimes life can be so painful and hopeless that one simply wants to end it. In the USA roughly 40,000 people take their lives each year. Sometimes, life can seem so completely entangled that it can appear impossible to untie the knots, but you must *never give up* just the same!

Imagine the sorrow you would cause if you were to commit suicide. By holding out you can save those around you from this burden. You can protect them from the hell they would experience in losing you. When you spin it this way, you are actually a hero for staying alive. Hold on to this thought.

Here is a supporting thought for those who wish to die: *What happens tomorrow?* The only way to find out is to hold out for one more day. You never know what tomorrow will bring, if it will be the day things turn. You owe it to yourself to wait one more day (and then another and another...).

If the great change still does not happen tomorrow, it still can be a good day. Maybe you do something fun, maybe the depression has decided to give you the day off. Maybe somebody new enters your life; maybe you eat a good meal or see a good film together with some friends.

You never know. It is impossible to predict. In addition, it is exactly life's difficulties that make the good moments valuable. Suffering defines happiness and vice versa. If you have reached a point-zero in life, a rock bottom where there is only suffering, everything above is a little better.

Because of the fact that some suicides are committed in the heat of the moment, it is wise to prepare an emergency number you can call if you are on the brink of taking your own life. Talk about it with people you trust, people who will not panic when you tell them about your suicidal thoughts. Make a pact with them that you will call them if it is truly serious. Acquire a list of which public agencies you can contact for acute psychological help.

Avoiding suicide has two parts, one acute and the other long-term improvement. It is vital to create strategies to avoid suicide in the heat of the moment. It is also important to work over time to improve your life situation such that you rid yourself of suicidal thoughts. The next part is about just that.

PART 4

LONG-TERM SELF-IMPROVEMENT

The process

If you have a problem, you must first *identify* what the problem is before you can solve it. This is the mapping phase in our model. In this phase you take a closer look at yourself in order to understand how you think, feel and act. When you understand more of why you act the way you do, you can *accept* the situation you find yourself in. Afterwards you can *decide* to change yourself in order to have a better life. Such a decision will make it easier to *implement* measures to go in this direction.

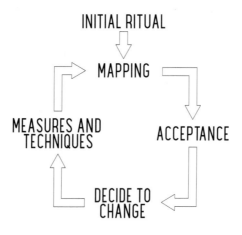

Afterwards you begin a new cycle of mapping, accepting and measures. I see self-improvement as a process which ideally lasts a lifetime. Make it a sport to become the best person you can be!

The goal of this is not to set out on some sort of witch hunt and cut out everything that is not perfect. If you were to do this (and if it was even possible), you would become a sterile and rather boring person. Who likes being together with "perfect" people who always do the right thing, and who never make mistakes? Perfection is an illusion; what is important is that you become a version of yourself who gets a little better at everyday life.

An initiation ritual

The first thing you must do is draw a line in your life – a divider, which marks the passage from a life as victim to a life as captain. This divider is created with the help of a simple initiation or transition ritual.

Here is one option: Choose a day you have off and get up relatively early. Take a shower. Tidy and scrub your home or your room. Go through your wardrobe and throw out any clothes that remind you of the life you have lived thus far. Buy some new, preferably colorful, happy clothes which *you* like. Throw away things which you associate with bad memories. Cut your hair in a new style. Changing style and appearance will reinforce and strengthen the effect of the changes you are about to make in your life. It will give you a daily reminder that you are in a process of change. If you feel like it, you can even get a tattoo which you associate with change or with the version of yourself you wish to be.

Next, take a trip, such as to a cabin or out camping. Choose a type of trip that promotes intense feelings as this will make the ritual more memorable. You can sign up for a guided rock climbing tour, conquer a peak, cross a mountain range or go through a forest. Try to find something that gives you the feeling of mastery, maybe something you have not dared to do before.

On the trip, eat healthily and drink little alcohol. Take along a diary so that you can note down your thoughts and reflections. When you return home, say for example on Sunday evening, your new life begins. Now you can take hold of everything you have been pushing ahead of you your whole life.

Mapping

The goal with the mapping phase is to understand yourself to the greatest degree possible. Understanding yourself is a considerable part of getting better. When you know yourself, you understand why you think like you think, feel like you feel and do the things that you do. You understand what triggers reactions, thoughts, feelings and moods. It is only when you know who you are that you can begin to change the way you think, and this will in time change your life. In the mapping phase you identify reality filters and demons as well as common thought fallacies. But you will also identify your strengths.

◊

Because mapping negative aspects of your life situation can be a difficult process, it is a good idea to begin by mapping your own *strengths*. People who are depressed typically do not focus on their strengths. They think unnecessarily often about what they lack and their weaknesses.

Mapping strengths is an important principle in positive psychology. Research has found that people can improve their quality of life by being aware of their own strengths and then building their lives around them. Building upon your strengths means that you form your life in such a manner that your primary strengths (also called signature strengths) are expressed as often as possible. If your most important strength is, for example, nurturing, you will find much happiness by seeking out jobs and situations where you can use this strength. A friend of mine changed careers, from interior design to nursing, quite late on in life because of this.

You can also attain this effect by seeking out areas outside the workplace where you can use your signature strengths.

We have multiple signature strengths. They can be blended together in many different combinations. If, for example, you have precision and creativity as your most important strengths and you work as an accountant, you can find expression for your other strength for creativity, by writing, painting or playing music in your free time.

How do you find your own strengths? It is likely that you already have a rough idea of what they are. You can find people who know you and ask them directly: *What would you say is my best trait?* If you are surrounded by critical people who cannot say anything positive, this would not be the best choice. Fortunately, there are other ways.

There are numerous tools on the Internet to this end. One of them may be found on the website *viacharacter.org*, a system designed by the world's foremost researchers in positive psychology. If you try this you are also part of a large research project, where the system anonymously gathers data about strengths in different people groups.

Finding your own strengths is closely related to mastering. People who are struggling with painful feelings can increase their quality of life by increasing their feelings of mastery. The easiest way of increasing feelings of mastery is by finding daily activities that suit your signature strengths.

Identify thought fallacies and reality filters

A core technique in cognitive behavioral therapy is called ABC, an abbreviation of the words *adversity, belief* and *consequence.* In my eyes ABC is the most effective technique to eliminate thought patterns which keep people down, and I would strongly advise you to try it!

During the course of the day we meet constant barriers and difficulties of varying intensity. For example, you buy a coffee at a cafe only to later find out that it is too bitter (*adversity*). You are already on the bus and it is too late to go back and change it. You think, *Argg! I am so tired; I really needed a good coffee. Why does everything have to go against me?* Here you are convinced that everything is against you (*belief*). The result is that you end up in a terrible mood, which makes your day worse (*consequence*).

When you have identified the A, B and C in an event or situation, you can then pose critical questions to yourself as to how you handled the situation, what you thought and felt, and which beliefs were connected to the experience. The core of the technique is analyzing beliefs and finding thought fallacies. If you perform ABC over a period of time, you will gain an overview of which thought fallacies you tend to repeat. These are the ones which must be eliminated.

Here is the method:

1. Describe the situation which occurred.
2. Describe the feelings you experienced during and after the situation.
3. Describe your thoughts during and after the situation.
4. Describe the beliefs you have which are relevant to the situation.
5. Identify the thought fallacies you were victim to during and after the situation.
6. Find alternative ways of relating to the situation which will be more beneficial to you.

You can use your journal for collecting this information. Alternatively, you can download the forms from my webpage, *kristianhall.com*. Here is an example of how the form may be used:

119

1. Describe the situation
   I was telling a story to a group at school, and the coolest person in class left right in the middle of it.

2. Feelings I experienced
   Humility, shame, embarrassment. Bad mood which then became depression.

3. Thoughts I thought
   I am not funny. I cannot tell stories. I cannot relate to others at all. I am a clown and no one likes me. No one will ever like me.

4. My beliefs connected to the situation
   Either people are funny and popular or they are not. Everyone else is funny and popular. I will always be a loser and will never have friends.

5. Thought fallacies
   Generalizing. Over-dramatizing. Mind-reading. Polarizing. Filtering.

6. Alternative, more useful thoughts
   There could be a thousand reasons why he left. Maybe he had an appointment. Other times I tell stories which make people laugh. It is not true that you are either funny or you're not.

Here is another example:

1. Describe the situation
   I had a date with my best friend. She cancelled an hour before we were to meet.

2. Feelings I experienced
   Rejection. Sadness which grew to full-blown depression.
   Shame.

3. Thoughts I thought
   She cancelled because she does not want to spend time
   with me. She does not like me. Nobody likes me. I am
   going to lose her friendship.

4. My beliefs connected to the situation
   This is a complete rejection of me as a person. The event
   was about me, not any external factor in my friend's life.

5. Thought fallacies
   Generalizing. Over-dramatizing. Personalizing.
   Mind-reading.

6. Alternative, more useful thoughts
   My friend has for years shown that she values me. Other
   friends have done the same. She cancelled the date simply
   because she was unable to meet (she said that she had to
   work because she had an important presentation the next
   day). It is fine if friends cancel appointments from time to
   time.

Training is required to master this exercise. If you find it difficult,
get yourself a few books about Cognitive Behavioral Therapy
(such as *Change your Thinking* and *The Resilience Factor*). You
can also meet with a cognitive behavioral therapist who is trained
to assist others with this and other techniques.

❧

You are already aware of many of your reality filters. You know
where you stand politically and religiously. You know which

121

core principles you hold. For example: *I always arrive on time for an appointment.* Or: *One should never lie.* Maybe you are also aware of a few of your deepest convictions, such as: *It is not possible to love me.* Or: *The world should be more just.* Or: *If I do not succeed in everything I do, I am a complete failure.* In the above examples you can see that reality filters can both be beneficial and detrimental. The subconscious parts of reality filters can be hidden like an iceberg below the water's surface, and can affect thoughts and feelings in ways you are unaware of.

Examples can be when you meet a barrier in your everyday life which leads to intense and disproportionate negative feelings, like throwing your cards to the floor after losing a game of poker, or when you experience a feeling which probably is not in accord with the experience, such as when you get angry when somebody walks away from you.

Other examples of this are when you experience contradictory feelings which stop you from making simple decisions, such as when you want to join your friends for a trip but there is something in you holding you back that you cannot put your finger on.

To identify *that which lies below,* you can start by using the ABC technique. When you have described the situation and the thoughts, feelings and beliefs connected to the event, you can use so-called Socratic questioning, a technique found in cognitive behavioral therapy which originates from pedagogy. The name has its roots in the Greek philosopher Socrates who was in the habit of standing on street corners and asking passers-by philosophical questions.

You can ask yourself the following questions:

1. What are the facts, and what is my own subjective understanding of this situation?
2. Which aspects of this situation support my subjective understanding?

3. Which aspects of this situation go against my subjective understanding?
4. Am I conducting any thought fallacies?
5. Which alternative, more positive perspective can this be viewed from?
6. Which other situations lead to similar reactions from me?

Here is an example:

1. Describe the situation as objectively as possible.
   I have a crush on my neighbor and have just invited her on a date. She said she couldn't because she is going on a trip. She said it might work next week.

2. What is my subjective understanding of the situation?
   Once again I have been rejected by a woman. I will never find a partner. I am not attractive. I will die alone. I will never invite someone on a date again.

3. Which aspects of this situation support my subjective understanding?
   She said 'no' to the date.

4. Which aspects of this situation go against my subjective understanding?
   She said that maybe she could meet next week.

5. Am I conducting any thought fallacies?
   Generalizing. Over-dramatizing. Polarizing. Mind-reading. Filtering.

6. Which alternative, more positive perspectives can this be seen from?
   She was open to the idea of a date after her trip. She did not say that she never wanted to go on a date. This was

not a rejection; it simply would not work this week. I can ask her again when she returns from her trip.

7. Which other situations lead to similar reactions from me? In other rejections, such as when friends do not come when invited.

❧

Demons (which are composed of different thought fallacies) can take the form of an inner, critical voice in your mind. They can, for example, say, *You are worthless, nobody likes you*. As we have explored earlier, most of the things this voice says to you are total lies. They are lies which are served with the purpose of putting you off balance, reducing your self-confidence and making you scared or unhappy. You can use Socratic questioning to expose the demons and reveal the erroneous logic which lies behind them.

So when the voice says, *You are worthless, nobody likes you*, ask yourself and the voice, *How do you know? Who does not like me? Where do you get that from? Who is it that thinks me worthless? Can I find an example of someone who has told me that they like me, and in so doing disprove these statements?* Continue to ask clarifying questions of this nature until you identify the thought fallacies and the implicit lies in the statement of the inner critic/demon.

Another example is manifested fear, such as *if I get on that airplane I will die*. Contradictory questions would be: *Why will I die? How many people die in airplane accidents each year? How large is this percentage of those who fly in total? How likely is it, then, that I will die?*

❧

I found another, more radical, method for identifying reality filters in Robert Anton Wilson's fantastic book *Prometheus Rising*. The method is concerned with using reality filters which you yourself do not hold, as though you are putting on a costume. By doing this regularly you will become aware that reality filters exist and of how they affect the way we think, feel and act. You will also be able to identify your own filters more easily. Let us take a closer look at this technique.

Next week you are to really embody the belief that the authorities across the world are behind a conspiracy to enslave the global population. Google words like *chemtrail, Bilderberger* and *Illuminati,* and pretend that you believe every word. Look for signs that indicate that the media is also in on this project. Really get into it! When the week is over, rid yourself of this reality filter.[5]

The following week you are to really believe that all people are good and that everyone wishes you well. Imagine vibrations in the air are manifested love. Believe that your health is improving every day. You can absolutely keep this reality filter once the week is over.

A shorter variant to this method is to choose two parties or social events you are to attend. This will be most effective if these events are close in time. At the first party you are to truly believe that you are as popular as a rock star, that you are the world's most attractive person, and that everyone around you wants to know you and spend time with you.

At the other party you are to believe that you are ugly, fat and stupid, that you are never funny and that absolutely no one wants to talk with you. If you are depressed *do not do this part of the*

---

5   If you suffer from, or have suffered from, psychosis or delusions you should not perform this experiment. The same is true if you regularly consume cannabis, LSD or other psychedelic narcotics.

experiment. It is likely that you already have a form of this reality filter, and you do not need further exposure to it.

Compare your experiences from the two parties (or of the first party and your life in general). If you succeeded in really living out the reality filter, you will understand what I mean when I say that these define how you feel, and that you can exchange these at will!

Simply observe

I found this method in the book *Taming Your Gremlin* by Rick Carson. The book uses a method for identifying and then defeating demons. The method begins with simply observing the demons passively and seeing what they do.

Carson's theory is that awareness of your demons and how they work will in itself result in their gradual loss of power. In other words, you are to live your life as usual, without doing anything in particular to rid yourself of demons, but be aware of how they affect your life. You even let them do what they want, like pushing you off balance or making you depressed, while you observe what happens. What you learn in this phase will provide invaluable information that you use later in the process. Use your journal to record what happens.

Instead of talking about a person's different demons, Carson collects all demons into one (which he calls a *gremlin*). This can be quite effective. You personalize the demons into one figure, which you can even name if you wish. Carson encourages that we visualize how the demon looks and describe it in detail.

You can take out a piece of paper and write down all of your negative thoughts, feelings and habits as represented in one simple figure. Try next to draw a picture of the demon. If it works better to draw several demons, that is okay too.

Try to work with a description and drawing of the demon(s) over time. Try to create the most accurate description of the demons and how they work – how they affect you, how they look, what type of voice they have and so on.

Brutal honesty

This chapter is especially important for those who have a tendency to blame powers and people other than themselves for what happens, or in other words, those who often use the thought fallacy of *blaming*. If on the other hand you personalize everything (which is the opposite of *blaming*), you should skip this chapter because you are already being brutally honest about yourself, and because you already amplify and warp your role in what happens to you. The point here is to find a balance and to understand that some problems, but certainly not all, are about who you are.

One problem with reality filters is that they can stop you from seeing things for what they actually are. This delusion then means you cannot see your own role in the situation. The victim role is a typical example of this: *Nobody sees me, nobody is nice to me, nobody loves me – and it is their fault.* The victim role is the manifestation of the thought fallacy *blaming*.

If you see life through such a lens you cannot take control over your own life, but instead reduce yourself to a powerless leaf floating on the river of life. Getting out of the victim role is crucial to improving your life.

Some self-help authors take this principle to the extreme. They say that it is completely impossible for other people to make you angry or sad. Others cannot provoke you; they cannot make a mockery of you. These are things that only *you* can do to yourself. If someone treats you poorly, you have a choice to make in how you will react. You can choose to not react at all, to not let others put you in a bad mood.

Deep down this principle is correct. Even if few of us in practice are able to control our own feelings to such a high degree that we do not let ourselves be affected by poor treatment from others, it is important to realize that we always have a choice. We can go from being powerless victims to being captains in full control of our lives.

When you are mapping what is wrong in your life and what would be advantageous to change about yourself, you must sometimes be brutally honest. Choose the right time for this exercise. If you are completely defeated it is best you wait until you have gotten over the worst of it.

Perhaps the easiest way to do this is to approach those around you (who know you well) and ask directly, *What can I change about myself in order to become a better person and have a better life?* Ask as many people as possible and jot down what they say. Try not to react right there and then, even if what they say is hurtful and provoking. Try to avoid self-defense mode, do not listen to the voice that tells you that they are lying, that it is not you who are the problem, that they are to blame (these are the demons talking). Simply note what they say. This exercise requires courage, but it can be extremely effective if you have difficulties seeing which changes would be advantageous.

At a later time you can look over your notes: What are the common features; what was said often? If many people have pointed out that one thing or another is your greatest weakness, it is likely that they are right.

Be kind to yourself in this phase, which may be the most painful in the entire self-healing process. You are standing in a phase where you must throw off your old self-image and replace it with a new one, where you have weaknesses, where things in your own mind are the problem. This can be very difficult. Go through this phase slowly, take one thing at a time and be kind to yourself. If you have any rocks in the people around you, hold tight to them. Tell them what you are doing and that you need their help and support.

Acceptance

Acceptance is an important milestone in the process of getting better. It is often after the acceptance phase that the real improvement can begin. In my opinion the point of acceptance is the true bottom in the curve for life happiness. If you manage to accept your situation and your own role in it (both good and bad), you are ready to continue on.

In order to improve yourself you must first accept your problems. For example, there are many people who are addicted to alcohol, narcotics, food or other things and who are not willing to accept their addiction. It is not a coincidence that acceptance is the first step of Alcoholics Anonymous' twelve-step method and of other related addiction groups.

If you are in a grieving process, you will not be able to move on until you have accepted the loss. It is completely okay if this acceptance comes after some time, but it is a critical milestone to accept that the one you lost is indeed gone and that this person will never return.

To demonstrate this acceptance to yourself and others you can communicate it, for example, by telling your friends and family (*I have accepted that I have a problem with alcohol*). Another way is to write it down in a journal.

Regardless of whether you ended up at an impasse due to your own choice or external factors, the most important thing is to realize that it is you who must take responsibility for the road ahead. Accepting this is an important part of healing.

Decide to change

Demons can have self-preservation mechanisms which make it difficult to free yourself of them. There are sub-routines in demons which maintain and amplify depression. The helplessness and apathy that accompanies depression is an example of this phenomenon, and it is extremely frustrating for those suffering and for the people around them. People with depression often let themselves fall behind, bills remain unpaid and accommodations remain untidy. The mental prison becomes less and less pleasant to sit in.

I believe that *anger* is the wagon that will take you out of the prison. For me, anger is raw and pure will, which holds so much energy that it can break down walls. So get angry! Realize that these demons have been holding you down for a long time. Let yourself explode (while not hurting yourself or others)!

Several studies of people who have managed great changes in their lives show that they simply reached a point where they said *enough is enough*. They reached a saturation point where they decided that they could no longer accept limitations in their quality of life and freedom. This is possible for you too. Simply decide that you are fed up, that enough is enough, that you want to go forward in life!

A family friend had for decades avoided going on trips abroad, despite actually enjoying these trips. The cause was intense fear of flying. One day he surprised his friends by meeting them at the airport. They asked him why he had suddenly decided to come along after years of declining. He responded simply, "I can't be bothered to fear flying any longer." After that he never had problems with his fear of flying.

You can make a symbol out of the point in time when you make the decision such as by writing down something like the following in your journal:

It is Monday the 14th of March, 2016, the time is 7:37 p.m., and I have decided to completely rid myself of depression. I will achieve this through a combination of cognitive behavioral therapy and techniques which improve my mood. Starting today I will use a gratitude journal and ABC daily.

For extra effect you can combine this with a ritual. You can, for example, describe your old self, what you are tired of and what you wish to rid yourself of. Then you can burn this note in the fireplace. Next write a new description – of the person you wish to become. This note is to be kept safe, or you can hang it someplace where you will see it every day.

You can use the following technique to amplify the feelings of disgust for the demons (it is important that your disgust is directed toward the demons and not yourself) until you attain the necessary critical mass.

Choose what you are tired of; let us say for the sake of an example that it is social anxiety. You are tired of always ending up as a wallflower in social groups, of never daring to speak with unfamiliar people. Imagine a fictitious or actual situation where the demon manifests itself, for example, the last time you were at a party and hid yourself in a corner. Intensify the image. By this I mean that you should zoom in on your fearful face and exaggerate the frightened expression. Imagine that you jump two yards into the air when a stranger approaches you, that sweat runs down your brow, that you hold yourself convulsively. Make an inner film about this characterized situation, where you are completely and disproportionately freaking out. Run this film with sound and music and sharp colors in your mind, again and again. Do this until you reach a level of loathing for the demon, until you

131

reach a critical point where you decide that this is ridiculous and that you want to make a change.

It is important that you maintain momentum after this. Surf the wave; use your freedom to make the changes you have always wanted to make but which you did not have the strength to do earlier.

Implementation phase

When you have mapped what it is you are facing, the next step is to make a plan for improving and then to implement it. A considerable portion of the plan will be to break the thought and behavioral patterns you have identified in the mapping phase.

Continue to use the techniques you have learned so far. This applies especially to ABC and Socratic questioning. Do

> *A combination of techniques from cognitive behavioral therapy and positive psychology will get you far.*

not let the demons rest, but expose them to an unbroken stream of critical questions. Continually search for thought fallacies, so that you become better and better at recognizing the warped and illogical thoughts which worsen your mood. I would recommend that you make this one of the main pillars of your plan.

Another main pillar can be the techniques associated with positive psychology. Constantly choosing activities and people who improve your mood is like continually taking a dose of good medicine. It is difficult for the dark side of the mind to gain a foothold when the body is full of signal substances connected to uplifting feelings.

❦

The demons will sometimes try to hinder your efforts to get rid of them. Imagine an overweight person who is trying to lose weight. One day he gives in and eats one or more chocolate bars. The voice in the head (the demon) says, *You see! You are weak and*

cannot even keep yourself from chocolate. Just eat more; you cannot control this; you are fat and ugly and nobody likes you!

When you are in the process of taming a demon, such as the overweight person's sweet tooth, one setback can make it difficult to get going again the next time. Self-confidence will often be reduced after a defeat, while it will increase

> Be prepared for setbacks; they are part of the healing process.

after each victory. I believe that the best way to avoid this effect is to *expect* and prepare for setbacks. You can include in the plan the fact that there will be setbacks, that it will be difficult, and that it can take some time.

Furthermore, it is important to be gentle with yourself when you fail. Think *oh well, I have countless new chances* each time you crash or have a setback. This can allow you to reduce the negative effects of the crash. A crash is not in itself a problem; it is the reduced self-confidence which is. Recall *Snakes and Ladders*: You may fall down from time to time, but in the end you always reach the goal.

It is wise to set up a strategy where you increase the odds of winning the daily battles against the demons and where you avoid the battles you will likely lose. In so doing, in time you will increase your self-confidence and become increasingly better at winning the battles. Try to avoid battles you know you will lose.

You can also plan in advance as to how you will react when you hit the ditch. We can use the weight reduction example again: Let us say that you are on a diet which avoids sugar. One day you cave in and eat an entire chocolate cake. In your previous life you would most certainly have become defeated and depressed by this failure. You would have beaten yourself up and further reduced your already low self-confidence.

But now you have planned how to react. You have decided in advance that you will not beat yourself up, that you will not make a big deal out of it, but simply resume your diet the following day. With this strategy the setback will not have any major

135

consequences. You will have maintained your self-confidence, and the self-improvement project may continue.

Willpower

The first step in training willpower is to realize that you have it. I have read the expression *the sick will* and think that it is a good one. People have a sick will when their energy level is at empty, when they can barely lift a finger, when all sorts of impulses can make them lose concentration. People with depression are the clearest example of people with sick wills. Here we can clearly see the demon's resilience and self-preservation. The depression has taken residence in the person and weakens their will in such a manner that getting out of this state can seem impossible to them. Some people lack an "immune system" against psychological illnesses; they must build it up from scratch.

Your willpower is your mental equivalent of white blood cells. I believe that we can see willpower as a muscle which can be lazy or well-trained. We must in other words exercise it: set up an exercise program, begin with small tasks and scale them up over time. To increase the feeling of mastery you can begin with simple tests of willpower. For example, take a 15 minute walk every day regardless of whether it is raining or otherwise uncomfortable. Once you have mastered one level, you can then gradually increase the intensity and degree of difficulty.

I train at refraining from chocolate. During certain periods of my life I have been entirely addicted to chocolate and eaten a large plate each day. Chocolate tastes good and to a degree it is healthy, but as with everything else in life, only in moderation.

Find whatever is 'chocolate' for you – something you indulge yourself in too often which it would be wise to limit. Do not choose something you are addicted to, like cigarettes or alcohol. These types of addictions are too serious to be suitable for willpower training. The purpose of this exercise is to increase willpower and mastery so that you can handle more serious demons later.

You can also do the opposite, or in other words find something which is healthy for you and which you currently do too little of, such as eat five fruits and veggies every day, or exercise two or three times a week. Remember that it is important to choose a level you actually can succeed at. Twenty minutes of brisk walking can absolutely qualify as exercise! You can increase the length, intensity and frequency later.

NLP

In the 70s Richard Bandler and John Grinder completed a pioneering psychological work. They wanted to find out what it was that really worked in therapy and studied the best therapists in California of the time to that end. The results of the study were collected under the umbrella term neurolinguistic programming, or NLP.

A core principle in NLP is to focus attention toward what actually works in order to cure psychological problems, rather than the cause to the problem (in this way it is similar to positive psychology). Because of this, NLP has been criticized by some psychologists who believe that this method only scratches the surface and fails to explore in-depth.

As I see it, NLP is a useful tool which can be used together with other methods for self-improvement, and preferably in combination with therapy. NLP includes techniques which will help you to take control over your thoughts and feelings.

Many books are written about NLP, and it is not my purpose to fully explore NLP here (nor is this possible). If NLP appeals to you, find some books for beginners, preferably written by Richard Bandler (some recommended books may be found in the reading list), who was one of those who invented it, or take a course.

Let me give you two examples of NLP techniques you can use beginning today to improve your life situation. NLP is among other things concerned with manipulating how thoughts and feelings are represented in the mind and body. Visualizing is used to a large degree. If you have little experience with these concepts, you may find it difficult in the beginning. The answer to this is simply to practice.

Immediate mood improvement

Close your eyes and imagine a memory which you experienced as especially happy, a memory which you exclusively associate with positive feelings. Choose a memory which brings forth intense feelings. For me this would be my wife and I in a sailboat one beautiful July morning a few years back. It is easy for me to recall that memory as I have photos of it.

Describe how you imagine this chosen memory. Is it a still-frame or a moving film? Is it in first or third person? In other words, do you see the memory as though you were experiencing it now, or like a movie taken by an external camera? Is the memory in color or black and white? Is there sound in the memory? Smells? Music?

Edit the memory in your imagination. If the memory comes as a still-frame, turn it into a movie. If the image is in black and white, turn it into color. If the memory is in the third person, change it to first person. Add sound, music and smell. Make the colors more vivid.

Associate a color with the experience of the memory, for example, yellow. Imagine that a cloud of this color (a brilliant yellow cloud) represents the happiness in the memory. Imagine that this cloud materializes around your feet, and that it then goes over your body, from your feet to the top of your head. Next, send the cloud down again. Repeat this process and let the cloud move itself over and through your body five or six times.

Note how your mood has already become better than when you began the exercise. This requires practice and can be difficult the first few times you try it. The point of this exercise is that by recalling a memory in this manner, you will bring out a part of those feelings you felt in the memory. When the memory is positive you will automatically become happier when conducting this exercise. You can use this exercise when you are irritated or sad in order to improve your mood. You can "sit" in the positive memory as long as you want; let it remain on your mental screen for a few minutes. You can also make a sequence of positive memories for increased effect by imagining several of them in a row.

Reduce negative feelings you hold toward another person

Visualize a person who irritates you, or a person you fear or have negative feelings toward. Describe the image of that person the same way you did in the previous example. Are you in first or third person? Is the image a still-frame or a moving film? Is it in color or black and white? Is there sound?

Next you are to edit the image, but in the opposite direction of the positive memory. If you are in the first person, go to third person. If the image is in color, make it black and white. If there is sound, take it away. If the memory is a moving film, turn it into a still-frame. Zoom out and make the image smaller on your mental screen.

Let the memory become a moving film again. Turn on the sound. Put a clown nose on the person. Make him or her speak with a Mickey Mouse voice.

Most people who try this method immediately begin laughing when the clown nose shows up. You have taken a person who brings out bad feelings and turned them into a clown with one simple mental exercise.

139

Mantra words and phrases

One central difference between thoughts and feelings is that the brain can handle only one dominant thought at a time, while feelings often operate as a mix of several elements, like grief and shame simultaneously, or even happiness and grief at the same time, also known as melancholy. To experience this in practice, try to calculate 13 x 7 in your head while you decide what you want to eat for dinner. The way I experience feelings is that they operate as colors which can be blended into different hues and shades, while thoughts as a rule operate one at a time.

You can therefore get rid of a negative thought process by replacing it with another, more positive one. Imagine your mind is a coffee mug. If the coffee mug is filled with mud you can clean it by rinsing the mug in enough fresh water. This is one of the reasons why I recommend doing activities which are most distracting when you are suffering emotionally – you exchange the negative thought process with something more neutral, or perhaps even something positive.

You can exploit this phenomenon by creating and using mantras. A mantra is a powerful thought impulse which works like a massive rinsing of the brain. You can use these to stop an emerging negative thought or feeling spiral.

Two of mine are *strength* and *trivial*. The former is used when I am about to do something I do not want to do, like eat more chocolate, or when I am about to get in a bad mood from some idiot in traffic. *Strength!* I mentally yell to myself. I roar the word, so loud that I almost jump.

The same applies to *trivial*. This mantra word is used when I find myself about to enter a bad mood due to something trivial, such as when my son has colored in one of my favorite books.

I learned the following mantra from Richard Bandler. It is especially effective when you want to silence the inner voice that tries to reduce self-confidence, or that reminds you of negative experiences. The mantra is simply: *Shut up.*

To increase the effect I usually add sound. I create an entire choir. Each time the inner voice tries to remind me about a mistake from my previous life which I can no longer do anything about, I turn on the choir: *Shut up!* it screams inside my head, and the inner voice disappears.

You can create your own mantra. It is a two-step process. First map out what you want to use this mantra for, where and when a specific demon attacks you. Next choose a mantra that suits the situation. Use this word each time the situation occurs. Roar it out mentally! For increased effect you can also add a visual aid. You can, for example, roar "strength!" while you imagine boxing gloves pounding away at the visualized demon. By all means use comedy – demons are rendered powerless by comedy. To get a visual example of the effect of this technique, check out the scene with the Boggarts in *Harry Potter and the Prisoner of Azkaban.*

♦

In addition to simple words, you can also create mantra phrases or affirmations, which in turn may become life rules. What is important with affirmations is that you must choose something *you actually believe in.* If you borrow another's affirmation and repeat it a hundred times while deep down you do not share the implicit philosophy, the chances are that the effect will be zero or even negative. Here is a list of affirmations to choose from, as inspiration to create your own:

Each day I am getting better and better.
This will also pass.
I can control my thoughts and feelings.
The world is what I make it.
Just do it!
Concentrate on what you can influence.
The future will shine if I do.

You can eventually make your own set of affirmations into a set of life rules, which will make it easier for you to make decisions and to prioritize what you do in life. Here are my life rules:

1. People and experiences are what count.
2. Material things are only important as a means to having more time for people and experiences.
3. I will have fun in life.
4. I will be supportive of those around me.
5. I will be a good person.
6. I will work to help others as well as protect nature and the environment.
7. I can improve my world by changing how I think.
8. I have a great degree of control over my thoughts and feelings.

If you combine these life rules with dedicating your life to something (as described earlier in the book) you will then have guidelines for making your life easier, especially when you are feeling down. It is like flying on autopilot: If something pushes you off course, you can concentrate on your life rules and what you have dedicated yourself to and this will put you back on the right course again.

A variant of this, one recommended by Stephen Covey in his book *The 7 Habits of Highly Efficient People*, is to write a personal mission statement. This is a short text, maybe only half a page, which describes the purpose of your life. By writing such a text you make plain what you wish to use your life for. If you are depressed, it would be advantageous to include elements such as helping others or working for a cause greater than yourself.

Catastrophe scale

This technique has been important during painful periods of my life. Nowadays I do not have to use it as often as it has become a subconscious habit. It is especially suitable for people who have a tendency to overdramatize whatever happens. The method is a perfect match to the thought fallacy over-dramatizing.

Visualize a scale from 1 to 100, where 100 represents your worst imaginable nightmare, such as losing your entire family in an accident.

Each time something unfortunate or negative happens, place this event on the catastrophe scale. Losing your job is quite serious and deserves a few points, maybe 10? To miss the bus, on the other hand, hardly deserves to register on the scale, even if it can be irritating right then and there.

This simple trick allows you to reduce the painful feelings that follow negative events. It allows you to see how little these irritating events actually matter. Using this technique, things which previously could have bowled you over will be reduced to a yawn. This is a fantastic technique, one that will eventually be integrated into your habits so that you automatically reduce your reaction to frustrating experiences.

People who survive an accident, lose somebody, recover from a serious illness and so on, will often re-evaluate their understanding of what is meaningful and what is not.

When someone dies, those left behind are left with grief. But for the acquaintances of those in grief, the death can surprisingly also have a positive function. This function is to promote a re-evaluation of what is meaningful. If you hear that a friend lost their son in a

> Whatever you ascribe meaning to has meaning.

traffic accident, would you not hug your own son extra tight the next time you see him?

Try to become conscious of the things which really matter, and the things which really do not. Many of us run around collecting material possessions and do not spend enough time with the people we care about. Find out what is important to you, and concentrate on that.

Exchange your inner voice

If you have inner voices when you are struggling emotionally, it is likely that the inner voices are pulling you down. If the voice says something like *You are worthless, nobody likes you* or *You are so fat* or *Well done, you sure made a fool of yourself there,* then the voice is a demon which must be fought.

One technique for achieving this is to simply exchange the voice. This is a fun way to train yourself to control your own thoughts.

Let us say that you made a mistake in the past, for example, that you drank too much at a party, and this resulted in you saying things that you regret. This has plagued you for years. Each time you are in a social setting, the voice says, *Come on, make a fool of yourself again like you did last time! You clown.* The voice does not relent and harasses you each time you are in a similar situation.

When this happens, you can do the following: First say *Shut up!* to stop the voice (as described earlier). Next, exchange the voice for another that you control. Make sure that the voice is friendly. Make it say supportive things, such as *Who hasn't ever drunk too much at a party and said things they regret? Who cares that you did that all that time ago? You have cleaned up your act and can drink in moderation. It is time to forgive yourself.*

After a while of exchanging the voice in this way, you will find that the inner critic increasingly disappears. It will gradually phase out and ultimately disappear entirely.

Using this technique, you take control over the thoughts you were previously a victim to. Remember this when you run into other demons that trouble you. If you can control or eliminate one, you can take them all out!

Another variant of this technique is to apply sound effects to your inner critic's voice. Make it sexy (quite comic), or make it talk with a Mickey Mouse voice. It is impossible to take seriously anything speaking to you in a Mickey Mouse voice. Try it.

Total submission

In some cases the demons will be so strong that they cannot be defeated with conventional tactics. But even in these situations there is hope. The twelve-step method used by Alcoholics Anonymous is an alternative when one is facing the toughest demons. The method has remained more or less unchanged for 80 years and has helped millions of people defeat addiction and other serious life problems

The main difference between the advice and techniques which I have provided thus far and the twelve-step method, is that the latter is concerned with submitting to a higher power. If you have tried long and hard to fight the demons on your own without success, you can seek help from a higher power.

Allow me to present a short summary of the twelve steps:

1. Admit and accept that when facing the demon, you are powerless.
2. Believe that there is a higher power which can save you.
3. Choose to submit yourself to this higher power.
4. Conduct a fearless soul-search of yourself.

5. Accept your weaknesses.
6. Let the higher power eliminate these.
7. Ask the higher power to help you.
8. Make a list of the people you have hurt.
9. Make amends with these people.
10. Continue soul-searching.
11. Improve your contact with the higher power through prayer and meditation.
12. Help others in the same situation to improve their lives.

As you see, the twelve-step method is very spiritual. It is easy to recognize much from Christianity in the program and I imagine that most of those who follow the program choose the Christian God as the higher power. This is, however, not necessary. In the book *12 Steps and 12 Traditions*, produced by Alcoholics Anonymous in 1952, this higher power can very well be the organization Alcoholics Anonymous.

Fake it until you make it

Most of us have an image of how we would be if we were free of our inner problems altogether. This is some form of ideal image that is quite different than when the demons are running the show. Such an image can be used as a weapon against the demons: By pretending that you are the ideal version of yourself, you will end up becoming more like the ideal. Fake it until you make it.

Fake it until you make it includes, for example, that you pretend not to be irritated until the irritation passes. It works! Research has found that people who force themselves to smile eventually become happier because activating the smiling muscles in the face releases endorphins.

So if it is 5pm, the children are picked up from daycare and your irritation is swelling because your husband has not emptied the washing machine like he said he would, put on a smile even if you feel like that is the last thing you want to do. Force yourself to smile and to not give him the rebuke you think he deserves. Do this until the wave of irritation passes.

◊

In my home we use a variant of *Fake it until you make it* which we call the *magical restart*. If there is a bad atmosphere and my wife and I are irritated with one another, one of us will say loudly, "Magical restart!" This puts in motion a predetermined act, where both of us must pretend we are in fantastic moods. We both begin by smiling and expressing positive comments like *What a great day it has been* or *That dress looks great on you*. Because this almost always brings about comical situations (two bitter people sitting at the dinner table and smiling – quite funny!), we usually start laughing. And once you have begun to laugh, you have succeeded in improving the atmosphere.

◊

Fake it until you make it also works in more serious situations. Imagine that you are sitting home alone and are feeling miserable. A friend calls, you pick up the phone, and he asks if you want to come along for a jog (or a beer). You are definitely not in the mood to meet people, to expose yourself to the risk of being depressed in public.

Go out anyway! Pretend that you are not depressed (it feels a bit like swallowing your emotions), plaster on a smile, and force yourself to joke and laugh with your friend. Do this until the depression passes or eventually becomes less intense. This works, but not always. You will likely succeed less in the beginning, but with practice you will be able to defeat many waves of depression using this method. It is absolutely an advantage if your family and friends know what you are doing, to support you and allow you to fail. If you know that you can go home whenever you wish, it is much less frightening to try.

Each time you succeed will make it easier the next time. It can be a good idea to start with easy demons, win in these situations and later move on to the more serious ones. Each victory will give you the feeling of mastery. Knowing you can control your own emotions provides a fantastic feeling of freedom.

Exchange your reality filters

Once you are aware of which reality filters you have, you can choose a new set of filters that are more beneficial to your life experience. I would recommend something along the lines of the following:

> I am a good person, I treat others well, and they treat me well in return. I regularly meet new and interesting people who like me and want to be together with me because I am an interesting person. Most everybody wish others well. We are all in the same boat, and if everyone simply realizes this, the world will be a better place. The world is on the right course because most people want the same thing – a better quality of life for all of the world's people and animals. I am a resourceful person; I can meet life's challenges and handle them in a good fashion. My health and humor is improving with each passing day. I believe that the world is full of love, and that I am bathing in this love with each and every breath.

If the words above do not work for you, write your own. Find out how you would see the world and yourself in order to maximize your happiness. Note this down in your journal or someplace else. You may need some time and several attempts before you get this right, but the process in itself will be useful and rewarding.

148

It may seem a bit crazy to simply trade in what you believe in. The only way to find out is to try it. You can pretend that you believe it is possible until you become convinced that it actually is. This is another example of using the *Fake it until you make it* method.

An aid in succeeding in this transition is to turn the Velcro/ Teflon effect upside-down (as described in the chapter about Reality Filters). Continually look for proof that your old reality filters are incorrect. At the same time, look for proof that the new reality filters are correct. If you go from believing *you can't trust anyone*, to *you can't trust everybody, but there are many you actually can trust*, take note each time a fellow human being shows that they are trustworthy. This will weaken the old conviction and strengthen the new.

Doing this will take you through the following development. I have included an example in italics:

Level 1: Being an unconscious slave of your own reality filters
I am depressed, the world treats me poorly, and nobody likes me.

Level 2: Being conscious that the reality filter phenomenon exists
I admit that there are people who are not depressed, but who are like me in other ways. For example, my friend who is not depressed, who grew up in a similar situation, acquired the same education and works in the same industry as me.

Level 3: Being conscious of your own reality filters
My friend thinks completely differently than I do. He does not, for example, take criticism personally; he doesn't take rejection from the opposite sex as a sign of something being wrong with him. I see that it is primarily the way I see myself and my surroundings that makes me depressed.

Level 4: Begin to replace your own reality filters
If I manage to see myself and my surroundings differently, I will be less depressed. I believe that I can learn much from my friend, try to copy how he sees himself and others. I will try this in the weeks ahead.

Level 5: Being aware that it actually works
When I have done this for a month, I am still sometimes depressed, but much less than before. I will continue the exercise.

Level 6: Permanently choosing the new reality filter which is more beneficial than the old one
Now I have gone a whole year, and I am working on fine-tuning my new reality filter. I have chosen to see people I meet as opportunities for fun and new experiences. I see myself as a person who has a tough background, but who is on the way to having a better life. I see that I actually can choose what I want to believe about myself and my surroundings, and that from now on I will consistently choose that which makes me feel better.

When you have mastered Level 6, you have become a master at controlling your own life. This may even be the only thing you need to do to have a much better life.

If you are struggling with this process, you can use meditation and self-hypnosis to get it moving. These techniques are the subject of the next part of the book.

PART 5

MEDITATION AND SELF-HYPNOSIS

Meet your subconscious

When measuring brain waves of children between the ages of 0 and 6, it has been found that most of the activity occurs at the so-called delta and theta levels, between 0.5 to 8 Hz. These frequency intervals are equivalent to those found in adults in sleep/unconsciousness and day-dreaming/meditation, respectively. Thus, children are relatively unconscious before they are 6 years old, and register experiences and impressions almost like a tape recorder.

At the same time important sub-conscious mental *programs* are created – reality filters which will significantly affect mental and emotional function-ality later in life. A child who experi-ences physical abuse or another form of abuse, will be injured by this and

> The way I see demons, they live in your subconscious and were born of painful experiences, especially those in childhood and youth.

may create demons in the process. Abuse is not always necessary; it can be enough to not be *seen* by your parents.

I believe that for the greatest effect one must battle these demons on the same wave length they were created on. This is why in some cases meditation, self-hypnosis or hypnosis will be necessary to rid yourself of them.

The short cut is to go to a hypnotist. While I absolutely recommend this, I will also encourage you to learn meditation and self-hypnosis. You will get an intro course in the next chapters. As I see it, meditation and self-hypnosis are the most effective tech-niques for personal development. You will receive the greatest effect if you combine techniques aimed at your conscious mind (such as those found in cognitive behavioral therapy or positive psychology) with techniques that work on the subconscious plane (meditation and (self) hypnosis).

Let go

What you will learn now is a simple meditation technique which I call the *Letting Go Method* (LGM). This is a common meditation technique, which is found in many variations. The most important source for me was *The Middle Pillar* by Israel Regardie. Using this technique will, over time, lead to less stress, more willpower, better sleep, improved concentration and better health. It is a very easy technique when it is done correctly and over a period of time. You can also use it to gradually change your mood for the better. LGM is a modular method which can be built up into several layers in order to achieve increasingly deep effects.

Step 1: Let go of thoughts and worries

Make sure that it is as quiet as possible around you, and that nobody disturbs you while you meditate. Turn off the TV and music, and turn off the sound on your telephone. Choose a time when you will not be disturbed. If you have an appointment immediately afterward, this will interfere with the effect because you will be left thinking about what you will do later. The perfect time is right before you go to bed or right after you have woken up. For late sleepers it is in the evening, while for early risers it is in the morning.

When all sources of distraction are eliminated, change into a house robe or something comfortable. Make sure that you are not too cold or too warm. Close your eyes. Begin to breathe deeply and slowly. This can be difficult or even uncomfortable in the beginning. In our hectic day-to-day lives we become accustomed to only breathing from the top of our lungs. Learning to breathe all the way down may be difficult at the level you are at now.

A good way to breathe deeper is to place a hand on your stomach and notice how the stomach expands upon the inhale and deflates upon the exhale. Because the lungs are surrounded by your ribs, changes in lung volume primarily occur downward, toward the stomach.

To help you breathe deeply and slowly, count inside your head. Try to concentrate only on the counting; this is in itself now the goal. Count slowly to four while you breathe in. Hold your breath while you count to two, and then breathe slowly out again while you count to four. Count to two while the lungs are empty, and then begin a new round by breathing in and counting to four.[6] Repeat this until you get tired.

The first few times you try this, your head will undoubtedly be filled with ideas, thoughts and worries. We are unused to not thinking about anything. The brain is like a machine, it needs some rest to maintain itself. When all of these thoughts come jumping into your head, you can simply *let go*.

You will need to do this a few times before you understand what I mean. Do not throw the thoughts out by force, but *let go* by concentrating on your breathing and counting. Imagine that your mind is wrapped in Teflon; no thoughts are able to latch on – they only slide away and disappear.

&

Do this little exercise every day for a few weeks. Consider the exercise as something positive which makes you more relaxed,

---

6 A variation of this exercise is to drop the two-second rest between inhaling and exhaling. In other words, you should breathe in while slowly counting to four, and then slowly breathe out while you count to four. Choose the variation that works best for you.

not as a duty. If you end up seeing it as duty, take a break and begin again whenever you find the desire.

By breathing correctly and letting go of worries, you have created a haven of the will where worries do not have power or influence over you. Fifteen minutes a day or a half-hour if you prefer, without worries can have a huge effect. You can increasingly take control of your life. This little exercise is an important step.

In time you will be able to stop, breathe deeply and say to yourself when something difficult pops up, *I can manage this, things will work out, just let go.* Then go straight to the worry: Solve the problem! After this, the worry will lose its strength. You control the worry, and not vice versa. You will note this shift in yourself by feeling tense muscles release at will. You will then fully understand what I mean by let go.

Step 2: Releasing tensions in the body

Enter a proper breathing rhythm by counting and breathing. Breathe slowly while you count to four. Hold your breath while you count to two. Breathe out while you count to four. Take a break before the next inhale while you count to two.

Next, focus your attention on your left foot. Breathe in, focus attention toward your foot, and breathe out while you think *I let go of my left foot.* In the beginning it can help to tense the muscles for a few seconds before releasing (this works for most but not all, of the muscles). This will provide you with a concrete experience of release.

The next body part is the left ankle. Do the same thing: Breathe in, concentrate on your left ankle, breathe out, and then release the left ankle. Continue this with the shin, knee, thigh and hip. Change to the right leg in the same sequence. Next the left arm: hand, wrist, underarm, elbow, forearm and then shoulder. Do the same with the right arm. You will note how all of the limbs are heavy, you feel almost like a person without limbs.

Next concentrate on the body, from the groin to the head, and move upward using the same technique. Divide the body into those parts which feel right: groin, lower stomach, upper stomach, heart, lungs, buttocks, lower back, middle back, upper back, collarbone, throat, neck and finally the head. Focus your attention toward the body part repeatedly if it feels tense. A typical example is the stomach; it is often tense. Try to focus your attention toward it, while letting go, until you feel the muscles release. This is a very pleasant feeling. It feels healthy, and it is. One often physically feels that the bloodstream once again has full access.

Sometimes you may experience something special when you get to the head. The body feels like a fountain of light and energy, which streams from the feet and out of the head. Sometimes it may go in the opposite direction. You can actually control this, but we will not go into such detail here. Do not be afraid if this happens to you. Let go, and let it happen.

What you are physically doing with this method is releasing the bloodstream in the various organs. The effect can be powerful. Sometimes dizziness or nausea may result. This will eventually disappear.

◊

LGM is effective against sleeplessness. When the body is completely relaxed and the mind free of worries, sleep usually happens by itself.

Sleep problems are often the result of imbedded fears of not being able to sleep and that have built up over the years. Ridding yourself of this fear is not done quickly. It may therefore be necessary for you to practice a lot in order to attain this effect.

Lie on your back, even if you are not used to sleeping on your back. Breathe deeply a few times, using the 4–2–4–2 method

157

described earlier. Do this until you are relaxed. Next go through the body parts while you release.

Try not to focus your attention on the fact that you are becoming more tired and relaxed because then you might suddenly think, *Now I am about to sleep!* and in so doing ruin the whole exercise. Concentrate only on correct breathing and releasing each body part. If you do not fall asleep the first time, try one more time and perhaps again after that, but do not try so many times that you become frustrated. Then it is better to give up for the night and rather try anew the next night.

Step 3: Heal yourself

In case of serious illnesses, acceptance of the situation and reducing the pain is often the main concern. But if you are suffering from a sickness which is not life-threatening, it is possible to use a variant of LGM in order to strengthen the body's natural healing abilities.

Everyone has heard of the placebo effect, of how people get healthier by taking a pill they believed to be medicine. The placebo effect can be summarized as follows: If you *believe* you are getting healthier, then you *will* get healthier. Unfortunately, the placebo effect has a nasty twin: the nocebo effect. If you believe you are becoming sicker, then you will get sicker.

The effect of belief on health is well-documented in science. Unfortunately, there are still people who mock this effect, doctors among them. We are stuck in a paradigm where people see the body as a machine, where doctors assume the role of the mechanic. This is obviously necessary in many cases, such as broken bones or heart transplants.

At the same time, there is no reason we cannot take the best from the mechanical approach while researching how to use the patient's own beliefs to increase the chances for improvement. If you would like to know more about this, I recommend you read the book *Mind over Medicine* by Lissa Rankin.

Take the following example: In a Japanese research experiment the researchers allowed a group of teenagers who were allergic to a stinging nettle-like plant to stroke this plant over one arm while stroking a similar yet harmless plant over the other. At the same time, they were told that the harmless plant was the one they were allergic to. Where did they react? You guessed it: on the arm stroked by the harmless plant.

Here is another example: The American surgeon Bruce Moseley wanted to research the effect of a type of knee operation in which he was an expert. He arranged for a classic double-blind test where half of the participants received a real knee operation, while the other half (control group) were tricked into believing they had received an operation. In reality, the surgeon simply had made a few cuts, which were then stitched closed again, and made sounds and movements as though it were a real operation. The result: the control group had exactly the same pain-reduction effects as those who received a real operation!

This implies that it is wise to work systematically with ourselves with regard to what we believe in so as to reduce the chance of becoming ill, and if already ill, to increase the chances of healing by focusing attention on our own belief of healing. For you who are depressed, this means that you must convince yourself that you actually can get rid of the depression!

If the first thought you have every morning is about your own sickness, or if you spend a disproportionate time, attention and energy worrying about becoming sick, then unfortunately the chances for getting better will be reduced; therefore, think *health,* not illness.

You can stand in front of the mirror every morning and say to yourself out loud: *Each day I am getting better and better.* Yet because this is primarily aimed at manipulating the conscious part of your mind and not the subconscious level, it will be less effective than doing the same thing in a state of meditation or hypnosis.

❧

Proceed as follows: Use steps 1 and 2 of LGM to calm your mind and body. Perform the breathing exercise and make sure that you have released all of your body parts. Continue breathing with the 4–2–4–2 rhythm until you reach a state of deep peace and relaxation.

Next, visualize that you are pulling in health-giving energy with every inhalation. Imagine that this energy is going to the part of your body where you need it. If you have a localized illness, such as arthritis in the shoulder, you can redirect the energy to where your illness lies. When you breathe out, you can imagine that the exhale carries the illness with it out of the body. When I do these exercises, I imagine that I am breathing in a bright health-giving mist, and that I am breathing out a dark smoke.

You can combine this with the repetition of a suitable affirmation, for example, *Each day I get healthier and healthier.* The effect of this exercise will be much greater if you believe that it will work.

If you are depressed, you can imagine a bright mist coming in with your breath and going up into your head, where it then pulls the dark smoke out with it when you breathe out. Visualize intensely that this exercise takes a little bit of your depression away each time you breathe out.

Self-hypnosis

Some people have prejudices against hypnosis. Almost every time I talk about my experiences with hypnosis and self-hypnosis, I am met with skepticism and sometimes even fear.

This really is not so strange. People think that hypnosis is about giving away control, that you are reduced to a puppet hypnotists can do whatever they want with.

This is not the case. Firstly, it is difficult to be hypnotized if you do not want to be. It is not the hypnotist who hypnotizes you, but you yourself. The hypnotist is simply the person who guides you into a trance. Nor can you be hypnotized to do something you do not wish to do. When people go on stage during a hypnosis show and do all sorts of strange things while hypnotized, they do this because they want to go on stage and get hypnotized. Every show-hypnotist spends time choosing the right participants, and the most important trait is their wish to be hypnotized.

When you are hypnotized and enter a trance, you remain conscious the entire time. It feels as though the conscious self takes a few steps back and leaves the scene to the subconscious. The consciousness becomes an observer, but an observer who has the ability to push the stop button at any time, to take you out of the trance. When you are hypnotized you hear all of the sounds in the background and are completely aware of what is happening around you. But at the same time the brain is operating at another frequency; when in a trance, you are very susceptible to changes in your subconscious mind.

Being in a trance can best be compared to being in a daydream. When you are sitting on a bus and your gaze drifts off because you are deep in a daydream, you are actually in a trance. This is also true when you have just woken up, but still have parts of the dream you have just left behind. When you have run far and are completely exhausted, you can also enter a trance state. In other words, trances and hypnosis are natural phenomena which we experience often. The difference is simply how deep you go into the trance.

❦

Self-hypnosis gives you access to the very operating system of your brain, the programs which direct the subconscious parts of yourself. Here you can remove parts of or entire programs; you can change them and re-write them.

The simplest way of performing self-hypnosis is to listen to a soundtrack you have recorded in advance. This has much in common with listening to a meditation CD. The content of the soundtrack is called a script. I usually record a script on my smartphone as this allows me to always have access to it, and I can then perform self-hypnosis anywhere I wish.

You can also buy pre-recorded soundtracks from professional hypnotists. This is a good way of accessing a professional script without having to pay the relatively high price of going to professional hypnosis therapy. However, a script will be most effective if you have written it yourself. You can custom make it so that it is as relevant to your situation as possible.

(Self) hypnosis has three parts:

1. *Induction*
    The induction serves the purpose of putting you into a trance. There are many different inductions, and you can make your own.

2. *Re-programming*
   This is the active part of the self-hypnosis, and it is in this phase where the changes to your subconscious occur.

3. *Exit*
   This is the shortest part of the self-hypnosis. The purpose is to take you out of the trance and back to a normal consciousness.

Here are some examples of sentences that can be a part of the script:

My health is getting better and better.

Each time I use self-hypnosis I go deeper into a trance and am increasingly able to affect my life for the better.

The migraines are getting smaller and smaller, the pain is disappearing gradually until it is gone altogether, and my health is getting better and better with each passing day.

I am getting calmer and calmer, less and less caught up in worries, and my sleep is getting better and better.

Be aware that the subconscious works a little like a computer; it registers things quite literally. You should therefore carefully examine what exactly you are asking for when you write a script. You get what you asked for. Here is an example: Let us say that you have written a script with the following text:

I am sleeping longer each night, and I am sleeping deeper each time I go to bed, so deep that I do not awake at the noises around me.

This may result in you not being able to get up when the alarm goes off. It is not very practical to wake up at noon when you have an important appointment in the morning. As I see it, this is the only risk with self-hypnosis – that you write things in the script that will be misunderstood, which will not help you.

Do not let this stop you from trying it out. A simple way of eliminating the risk of undesirable effects is to get someone you know to carefully read the script before you use it, preferably somebody with some language skills. A script is like a computer program or a legal contract; it requires precise language. Alternatively, you can pay a hypnotist to write and record a script for you.

The complete self-hypnosis process is as follows:

1. *Get a script*
   You can buy pre-recorded hypnosis soundtracks online, or contact a professional hypnotist. If you only want to try it, you can use the example in Appendix B. In this case you simply read the text into some recording device (or your phone if you have this function). Make sure that the script includes all three parts (induction, reprogramming, and exit phase) of the hypnosis process.

2. *Use LGM to enter a relaxed state*
   Sit yourself in a comfortable chair or lie in your bed. Go through steps 1 and 2 of LGM. Achieving a trance will be easier and deeper if you are completely relaxed.

3. *Play the soundtrack*
   The rest is automatic. Simply listen to the soundtrack while you relax. Concentrate on the soundtrack; the effect is reduced if you think about other things.

This is one of the advantages with self-hypnosis. It is a passive procedure; all you need to do is relax and listen to the recording. Self-hypnosis provides an additional bonus as well: it provides you with a *power nap*.

Make sure that you never listen to a hypnosis track when you are occupied with other things, such as driving a car or operating machinery. Ensure that you remain undisturbed for as long as you listen to the recording. Some ideas for suitable times: in the morning (if you are a morning person), as a part of your lunch break, after work or school, or in the evening. If you have problems getting to sleep, it may be beneficial to use self-hypnosis in the evening and include a sentence which makes you tired. It does not matter if you fall asleep in the middle of the script. The only disadvantage is that you lose the effect of whatever plays after you have fallen asleep. You cannot be hypnotized while you sleep.

❦

If you want to maximize the effect of self-hypnosis, write your own script and work on it over time. I have a MS Word document which I continually update. When I have changed the document, I make an audio recording with my phone.

You can begin like the example in Appendix B, but change the sections that are not relevant to you. You can add as many sections as you want. When you record the script, take your time and talk in a deep and slow voice, while at the same time varying your intonation to emphasize especially important sentences and words. There are numerous good books on self-hypnosis, and if this works for you I recommend researching this further.

From my experience, I find that it helps to listen to a self-hypnosis recording every day for a few weeks before the effects become noticeable. Try at least to repeat the procedure every day for a week.

Continual self-hypnosis

It is important to be aware that you do not need to sit in a chair and listen to a recording to do self-hypnosis. In fact, we do this unconsciously all the time. And when we do it unconsciously, we do not have control over what we include in the script.

If you have ever said things to yourself before like: *I never succeed at work* or *I will never find a partner*, these are examples of continual negative self-hypnosis. If you continually tell yourself that you will never find a partner, it will likely become true. As car magnate Henry Ford said, "If you think you can do a thing or think you can't do a thing, you're right."

Those who suffer from depression will as a rule go around in a state of constant negative self-hypnosis: *I will never be happy. Nobody likes me.* In my case I said things like *I am not funny* and *I will never find a woman.* I do not say this any longer.

Unconscious self-hypnosis works like a constant reminder of, and amplifier of, the reality filters you possess. If you wish to change reality filters it is important that you change what you say to yourself.

Fortunately, we can control this phenomenon. When you know what you usually say to yourself, you can use the mantra word technique to stop it. Each time you think a negative self-hypnosis thought, you can roar *Stop!* with an inner voice and immediately replace the negative thought impulse with something positive. If you have told yourself, *I will never find a partner*, stop it and begin saying, *Any day now my dream partner will be right around the corner.*

Turn this into a habit and say things such as *Every day my health is getting better, I am getting increasingly better at controlling my thoughts and feelings* or *I am becoming more and more attractive to potential partners.*

Go ahead and make a sign with your selected self-hypnotizing expressions, and hang the sign on the bathroom door or in your bedroom so that it is the first thing you read each morning and the last every evening. Alternatively, you can tattoo them on your underarm so that you see them all of the time, but in this case you should really think through the exact words. Tattoos are, after all, permanent. It is also nice to not have to explain a tattoo to everybody who asks.

Since we are endeavoring to create our own reality, on the material, psychological and metaphysical levels, what you think and feel will gradually be transferred into your reality. Take control of what is happening to you!

Visualization

Visualization is a powerful tool which is closely connected to rituals, and which uses the same underlying phenomenon used in self-hypnosis. With the help of visualization you can contribute to forming your future and eradicating barriers.

An important aspect of visualization is to force the mind to see the possibilities in a situation, not the limitations. *What you give meaning has meaning.* Visualizing is concerned with using the placebo effect so that you achieve what you want.

You will get *much* more out of visualizing if you actually *believe* in the technique. If you do not believe, you can teach yourself to *(fake it until you make it)*.

The brain cannot discern between imaginary and real impulses. If you wholeheartedly visualize your greatest fear, your pulse will increase and your skin will begin to sweat, while the glands in your body produce stress hormones. This is exactly the same process that occurs inside your brain when you visualize, like when you experience something in the real world. This is the reason competitive skiers spend so much time visualizing the track they are about to ski through.

Numerous research experiments have found that it is possible to increase the body's muscle mass by visualizing weightlifting. Researchers have measured nearly equal improvement in the ability to play a piano piece by practicing mentally as if sitting in front of a piano. This phenomenon can be used to your advantage.

❧

Let us try visualizing: Use LGM to enter a positive state; in other words, you are completely relaxed and have let go of the day's stress and worries. This may be experienced as your own little safe room. It is here that you are to lay the foundation for your future improvement.

Think about the thing you wish to change. This can be any of your wants, dreams, fears or worries. Let us say that you wish to make the best possible impression at a job interview the following day.

Close your eyes. Imagine that you are sitting in a cinema where you have a huge screen in front of you. The screen fills your entire field of vision. The visualization is shown on the screen like a movie, but like a 3D movie where you not only see the film, but also live in the film. You see all of the images and the movie in the first person, as though you were the camera.

Imagine that you are sitting in the interview. Use lively scenes with color and sound. Imagine that you are radiating with self-confidence. Imagine that the interviewers are laughing out loud at your jokes, and that they are thinking, *This candidate is the one for us!* Let this scene move on to the left. Create a new scene, this time of yourself signing the contract for the job. Everyone around you is smiling, and most of all you as the conditions of the job are quite good. You know that you will do a fantastic job and that the position is perfect for you. Let this scene pass to the left. Imagine a third and final scene. In this scene you have begun the new job. Imagine that you enjoy the respect and trust of your colleagues. They laugh at your jokes; they admire you for the work you do. Fill in positive details that suit just your situation.

Here is another example: Imagine an image of yourself where you are lying in a bed, full of dark thoughts. This image can be a still-frame in black and white. Let the image pass to the left. In the next sequence, which is a motion film, you visualize that you have begun working on the way you think, in such a way that you produce uplifting feelings. Let this sequence pass to the left. Finally, you create a final sequence where you are smiling and are happy, and are surrounded by people you care about. Imagine that you have mastered things you previously could not do, like being popular at a party. Let this sequence linger a moment on your mental screen until you let it fade out. Make sure that there is sound during the scenes, that you experience them in the first person, and that they contain energetic and harmonious music.

Some people would say that what you are doing with this exercise is pushing the odds in your favor at the quantum level (as in quantum physics). Alternatively, we can call it pure psychology. If you manage to convince yourself that you are a fantastic candidate for the job, or that you will succeed in getting rid of depression, you increase the chances that it will happen. It is yet another form of self-hypnosis.

This method can be tailored to a wide variety of situations. If you are sick, the technique can be used to increase the chances that your own immune system defeats the sickness (depending on how serious the sickness is). Or you can use this technique to gain increased self-confidence before a date.

Your ideal self

I learned this technique from the British hypnotist Paul McKenna. You can read his book *Change Your Life in 7 Days* for further details. It is a form of visualization that increases the chances of achieving what you want in life.

Begin with LGM, and make sure that your body and mind are relaxed and that you are free of worries. Close your eyes. Imagine another version of yourself standing before you in the third person. This is the most perfect version of yourself you can imagine. Visualize all of the details: how you are standing, what expression you have and which clothes you are wearing. Visualize this in moving pictures, in other words, so that you see a film starring you. Add colors, sound and smells if you can.

Visualize how the ideal you relates to the world. How do you handle problems and challenges? How do you relate to other people? Do you smile and laugh? How is your body language? What does the perfect day look like to this version of you? Imagine an entire day for the ideal you. Visualize how you wake up (where do you live?), eat breakfast and meet any family members. If you are single and looking for a partner, visualize your perfect match. Imagine how you go to work, how you conduct your job, and so on.

Then take a step into the first person role of your ideal self, as though you put on this person like a garment. Imagine what your ideal self says, hears and feels. Conclude the sequence by daydreaming about how it would be to live the life of the ideal you.

Use this visualization every day for a week and observe the effects. If it works for you, you can integrate it into your daily meditation or self-hypnosis routine.

Rituals

If you put on your social anthropologist glasses and take a look at the world's cultures, you will find a number of common traits. One of them is that all cultures have rituals. This is because rituals have several important functions.

With regard to this book's theme, transition rituals are the most relevant. People have these rituals because they make the great transitions in life easier and more notable. A good example of a transition ritual is a funeral. The funeral is an important part of marking the end of a life. Without a proper burial, those grieving will have greater problems dealing with the loss. We need a grave to visit, a mark over the dead.

Rituals can be used in all difficult transitions including when overcoming demons. When my sister was going to quit smoking and had her last cigarette, we had the following spontaneous transition ritual: We danced a happy dance in her apartment before we burned the last pack of smokes in the fireplace.

Dancing a happy dance is not for all, but if you are going to stop smoking you can burn the last package and watch your last cigarettes disappear.

Here is another example that can be useful in connection with a loss or a split: Write a letter to the person who is no longer in your life. In the letter you can write about the grief you feel and the love you had for the person, and possibly the anger you feel about a specific event in the relationship. Write about the unfinished aspects of the relationship you had with the person who is gone.

If the person hurt you, you can write that you forgive them. If you were the one who hurt the other, you can write this down and ask for the person's forgiveness. When you are finished with the letter, you are to release it. You can bury it in the ground, or wrap it around a piece of bark (or a wine cork) and throw it in the sea (make sure the letter is anonymous so that it cannot be traced back to you or the person you write it to). As you release the letter, you are to visualize that you physically and emotionally are letting go of the feelings you have described, and that you completely accept the loss of the person or the relationship.

Immerse yourself

The way I define *flow* is the state where almost everything is working as it should: when things you have dreamed of or wished for a long time suddenly materialize, when your plans become a reality, when people around you – and yourself – have good feelings.

An image of flow is when the chaos in the world suddenly turns into an organized system, where all of the bricks fall into place before you, where the jungle reveals a trail you can follow. When you have flow, you forget time; you simply *are*.

I believe the path to flow is through systematically working with the barriers we have in life, barriers at the physical, mental and emotional levels. Gradually depression, frustration or anxiety will become less intense and be replaced by happiness and expectation. This is attainable for everybody.

Today many people still ask the age-old, greatest question: *Who am I? What am I? What is reality?* If you want to find an answer, you can ask those who explore this daily. I am not thinking of various types of clergy who would likely try to convince you with their own dogmatic view on the matter. I am thinking about physicists.

For hundreds of years people believed that the world worked like a giant clockwork (thanks to Newton). This means that the world is deterministic, or in other words, everything that happens is predestined, which means that there is no free will, that we are all robots without self-control.

Werner Heisenberg put a solid stop to this view in 1927. His so-called uncertainty principle says that we cannot calculate the properties of an atom. The atom is one of the building blocks

175

for everything in the universe, including you and me. It is simple logic to take this principle to a higher level: If you cannot predict with certainty the properties of an atom in the next second, you certainly cannot predict what you and I will do with our lives.

In the 70s the British physicist John Bell came with his pioneering theory. Bell's theorem postulated that everything in the universe is affected by so-called non-local causal effects. You have maybe read about twin particles in a science magazine; this is an example of Bell's theorem in practice. In simple terms Bell's theorem means that things in the universe, or the world, which are very far from each other, can affect each other without being in physical contact. In other words, everything can be, or is, connected to everything, regardless of distance. From this it is not a big step to argue that *everything is one*. For me this means that we are not alone, ever – that nobody is fundamentally lonely and alone. For me this is an endlessly beautiful idea.

The most meaningful thing in life for me is love. If you dig down deep enough you will reach the bedrock, and this is made of love. Love is not sugar-sweet; it is smooth as velvet. For me this is the very answer to the eternal questions: Who am I? What is this? What is reality?

The mainstream interpretation of quantum physics (The Copenhagen Interpretation) sounds like Buddhism: The world is an illusion which is made by its observers. The world acts only as a tendency, but then collapses into a concrete form when it is observed. In other words, *you* create your own universe, and the only real world for you is created by you yourself.

If we depart from quantum physics and look instead to psychology, we receive the same picture. Our understanding of the world is composed of sensory impressions which are *interpreted* in our brain. We are never in direct contact with reality; we experience an interpretation of it, a model or a map. And it is either we or the demons who decide how these impressions are to be interpreted. If we manage to rid ourselves of the demons, it is *we* who decide how our world should be interpreted. And if we

176

decide how it is interpreted, and the world is how we interpret it, this means that it is essentially us who decide how the world will be – in other words, how the world *is*.

We are the creators of our own reality. You can form your own world and in so doing form your own happiness. I wish you the very best of luck!

Every man and every woman is a star.

– Aleister Crowley

Thank you!

There are many people to thank in connection with the release of this book. I would like to begin with those who have been directly involved in the production process: A large thank you to my editor, Anne! We have had tough discussions regarding both structure and content, and there is no doubt that the book has become much better thanks to those discussions. Thank you, Thomas, for the fantastic illustrations, including the cover page. Another big thanks to the translator of the book, Jonathan. It's been amazing to see my own words taking form in another language.

I will also direct an emphatic thank you to those who have gone through the book and provided feedback regarding the psychological theory. Thank you, Hedvig, who is a psychologist, and my cousin Elsebeth, who is a psychiatrist.

It has taken me a long time to write this book, and it has not always been easy to keep up my motivation. Therefore, I thank my sister Henriette and my beautiful wife Kirsten for their continual moral support! Kirsten, who is also a psychologist, has in addition provided important input to the content. A thank you to my mother for her unshakeable belief in me, always.

Thanks to all of my friends, who together with my family make life the adventure it is! A special thank you to Harald, who came up with the title, publishing house name, and much good input for the text. I would also like to thank Hansi, Henning, Isak, Vidar, Wilfried, Johan, Petter, Helge, Espen, Alvar, Lars, Henrik and Gaute for all the good conversations which have created the basis of this book.

Finally, thank you to all of you who read this book! You are the reason I have sat in front of the keyboard all these hours. If you have any feedback about the book, I would love to hear it. You can send me an email at *post@kristianhall.com*. I would also appreciate it if you would leave a review at the place you bought the book, such as amazon.com.

APPENDICES

Appendix A: Further reading

The goal of this book was to write a starter-book of sorts, a book which could inspire you to continue along the path to a better life, and which could point toward other useful resources. The following is a list of books I whole-heartedly recommend. The more you read about getting rid of depression, the easier it will be.

Self-development
Feel the Fear and Do It Anyway – Susan Jeffers
The Worry Cure – Robert Leahy
Taming Your Gremlin – Rick Carson
The Power of Now – Eckhart Tolle
The 7 Habits of Highly Efficient People – Stephen Covey
Get the Life You Want – Richard Bandler
The Structure of Magic, Vol. 1 – Richard Bandler, John Grinder
Evolve Your Brain – Joe Dispenza
Flourish – Martin E.P. Seligman
Step-By-Step Tai Chi – Master Lam Kam-Chuen
Clear Your Clutter with Feng Shui – Karen Kingston
Change Your Life in 7 Days – Paul McKenna
Mind over Medicine – Lissa Rankin
Breaking the Habit of Being Yourself – Joe Dispenza
Positive Psychology for Overcoming Depression – Miriam Akhtar
Change Your Thinking – Sarah Edelman
The Resilience Factor – Karen Reivich and Andrew Shatté
Flow – Mihaly Csikszentmihalyi

Metaphysics

Prometheus Rising – Robert Anton Wilson
Quantum Psychology – Robert Anton Wilson
The Field – Lynne McTaggart
The Tao of Physics – Fritjof Capra
What the bleep do we know – William Arntz, Betsy Chasse, Mark
Vicente and others
Science and the Akashic Field – Ervin Laszlo
The Holographic Universe – Michael Talbot
The Middle Pillar – Israel Regardie

Fiction

Narcissus and Goldmund – Hermann Hesse
Steppenwolf – Hermann Hesse
Siddhartha – Hermann Hesse
Buzz Aldrin, what happened to you in all the confusion? – Johan
Harstad

Appendix B: Example of self-hypnosis script

In order for you to begin self-hypnosis right away, I have included the following examples of self-hypnosis scripts. You can use the script as it is, or you can make changes to "hone" the script to your own situation. Read the script aloud into a recording device or smartphone, and listen to the recording when you want to test self-hypnosis. It is as easy as that.

IMPORTANT: Only use self-hypnosis when you are in a situation which has no risk of dangerous consequences. For example, do not listen to these recordings while you drive a car or are otherwise in areas with traffic. Be extra careful with self-hypnosis if you suffer from epilepsy or have experienced psychosis. If you are unsure, consult your doctor.

Self-hypnosis script

You can close your eyes at any time. You are on your way into a trance, a hypnotic state which will help you become the best possible version of yourself. Imagine you are entering a beautiful forest. Look around you at the beautiful trees, the green moss. Breathe in the fresh air. Feel how the fresh air makes you feel well. Imagine the trail you are walking upon, the textures of the bark on the trees. You go deeper into the forest as I count to 10.

1–2–3–4–5–6–7–8–9–10.

While you go through the forest, you see an opening. You go into the opening. In the opening is a cozy little red cabin. You open the door to the cabin and go in. Inside the cabin there is an elevator. You enter the elevator and push the button for the lowest floor. The elevator goes down while I count to 10.

1–2–3–4–5–6–7–8–9–10.

When you leave the elevator, you see that you are in a large cave, where many tunnels go in different directions. You choose the one which appears to go the farthest downward. You go down the tunnel while I count to 10.

1–2–3–4–5–6–7–8–9–10.

Now you arrive at a new cave, lit up by beautiful luminescent algae. In the middle of the room is a throne. It is your throne. When you sit on the throne, you have all power over yourself and the things at your disposal. You sit upon the throne.

You are now in a state of hypnosis, which will become deeper and deeper as you listen to my voice. When the session is over, you will wake up rested and clear. If it is evening now and you are soon to go to bed, you will sleep naturally and quickly, and sleep well through the night. And now my voice will go with you.

You feel how your body becomes increasingly relaxed. You can find the most relaxed part of your body and experience how it feels. You can let that relaxed feeling spread from this body part to the rest of your body, like a warm, comforting wave. All muscle tensions are released. All pain disappears like mist before the sun.

Your sleep becomes better and better. Because of this you will enjoy an increasingly optimal energy level and better mood, which will allow you to do the things you want to do.

The quality of the self-hypnosis is improving. You are going deeper and deeper into a trance, and the effects of the positive self-improvement are gaining depth.

You are completely aware of what you want to do in your life. Your relationships will gradually improve, become deeper and closer. At the same time, you will continue to attract new, fantastic people, who contribute good things to your life. They will also help you achieve your goals.

Your health is getting better. Now that the negative stress is gradually disappearing, until it has completely vanished, the body's own systems will make sure that you have and maintain good health.

Your mood is getting better. You will gradually become happier, and you experience that you are largely happy and satisfied with life. You smile and laugh more and more. There is no reason not to smile and laugh.

In the brain and the body there are a myriad of small factories, which are capable of producing the substances you need to become happier. You know this deep down. You realize that your own body is able to produce the substances that make you happy, much happier than you have ever been before. You note how these factories listen to my voice and have now already begun the production of the substances you need most. You see that you are well underway on the journey to a happier life and a lighter mind.

In the same way you will gradually become more and more effective in working toward your goals, and you will find great happiness in working purposefully and effectively toward that you wish to achieve. You can easily ignore the potential distractions, which are disadvantageous.

Be aware that your subconscious will continually find effective paths to your goals. I ask your subconscious now to use its enormous wisdom to find the best solutions for you, so that you may reach your goals, and you will become more light hearted.

Now I will count slowly to five, and you will gradually wake up and come out of the hypnotic state. When I have reached one, you are fully awake and ready to continue the work of attaining your goals. If it is late in the evening, you will fall asleep quickly when you go to bed, and sleep well through the night. If you need to wake up during the night for whatever reason, you will manage this without any problem.

5 – 4 – you awake slowly – 3 – 2 – you can stretch and yawn if you want – 1 – you are completely awake.

Appendix C: Endnotes

1   In psychology there are two schools regarding how to view depression and other psychological illnesses. One school contends that either you are depressed, or you are not. The other considers psychological illnesses on a scale, for example, that depression can occur from simple blues to intense depression including suicidal thoughts. I share the latter view. I believe that it is often the same mechanism which is behind mild and serious cases (and that the most important difference is the intensity). This is the reason I decided to write about both small problems, like persistent irritation, and serious problems, like suicidal thoughts, in one book.

2   Recent research in the field of epigenetics (which means "above the genes") finds that genes in themselves do not necessarily decide your health or which traits you have. Genes function like a library and are activated by substances which are sent from the brain and other organs. This is important because it means that there is no genetic determinism (fate), a paradigm science has lived with for several decades. In other words, it is not a given that you will develop a sickness you are genetically susceptible to. This research hints that we have a much larger influence over our lives than we have previously believed, and this is truly something to celebrate!

3   Something which is less well-known is that the heart has its own "brain", which is made of several tens of thousands of nerve cells. The old mystical expression to think with your heart gains a whole new meaning.

4   Here people can be very different. Many do not have voices in their head at all. Others have inner dialogues which are manifested as voices in their head. Some have critical voices, which I describe as demons in the cases where they work against you. These voices often sound like one's own voice. On the other hand there are people who hear voices from external people (sometimes even from famous figures like Jesus or the devil) in their head – in other words, voices that are not their own. They will often be diagnosed with schizophrenia.

About the Author

Kristian Hall went through eleven years of deep depression as a teenager and student. He overcame his depression by practicing techniques from cognitive behavioral therapy and positive psychology. His personal development did not stop there – he's now living the life of his dreams. He lives in the deep forest around Oslo, together with his family and a very strange Maine Coon cat.